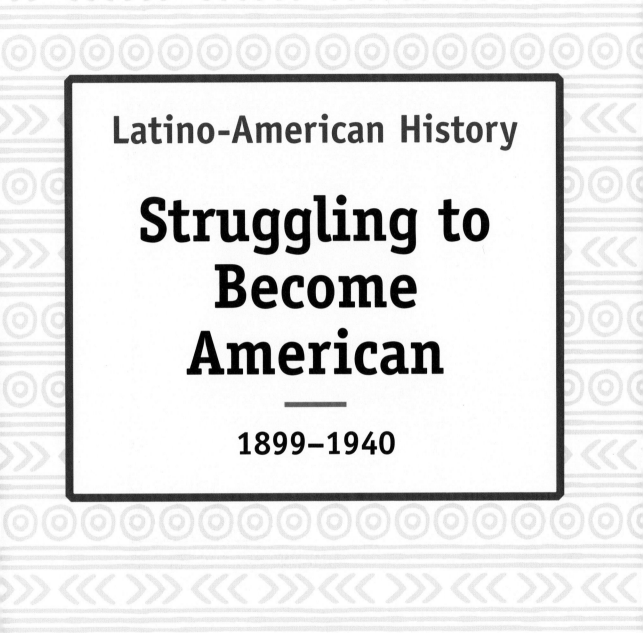

Latino-American History

Struggling to Become American

1899–1940

Latino-American History

The Spanish Conquest of America
Prehistory to 1775

Independence for Latino America
1776–1821

Spanish Settlement in North America
1822–1898

Struggling to Become American
1899–1940

Fighting for American Values
1941–1985

Creating a New Future
1986 to Present

Latino-American History

Struggling to Become American

—

1899–1940

by Robin Doak

Mark Overmyer-Velázquez, Ph.D., Consulting Editor

CHELSEA HOUSE
PUBLISHERS
An imprint of Infobase Publishing

COVER *A New Mexican home is built using bricks of adobe in July 1940.*

Struggling to Become American

Copyright ©2007 by Infobase Publishing

For information contact:

Chelsea House
An imprint of Infobase Publishing
132 West 31st Street
New York, NY 10001

Library of Congress Cataloging-in-Publication Data
Doak, Robin S. (Robin Santos), 1963-
    Struggling to become American / Robin Doak.
        p. cm. — (Latino American history)
    Includes bibliographical references and index.
    ISBN 0-8160-6443-1 (hardcover)
    1. Hispanic Americans—History—Juvenile literature. 2. Hispanic Americans—Cultural assimilation—Juvenile literature. 3. United States—Ethnic relations—Juvenile literature. I. Title.
    E184.S75D63 2006
    973'.0468—dc22
2006017140

Chelsea House books are available at special discounts when purchased in bulk quantities for businesses, associations, institutions, or sales promotions. Please call our Special Sales Department in New York at (212) 967–8800 or (800) 322–8755.

You can find Chelsea House on the World Wide Web at **http://www.chelseahouse.com**

Cover design by Takeshi Takehashi

A Creative Media Applications Production
Interior design: Fabia Wargin & Luis Leon
Editor: Matt Levine
Copy editor: Laurie Lieb

Photo Credits
© CORBIS page: cover; The San Antonio Light Collection, UTSA's Institute of Texan Cultures, #L-1541-D, Courtesy of the Hearst Corporation page: vi; Library of Congress pages: 8, 14, 18, 34, 45, 62, 65; The Granger Collection, New York, pages: 12, 24, 70; Mexican photographer (20th century)/Private Collection/The Bridgeman Art Library page: 26; The Bridgeman Art Library page: 29; © Private Collection/Peter Newark American Pictures/The Bridgeman Art Library page: 31; North Wind Picture Archives page: 38; © Christie's Images/The Bridgeman Art Library page: 42; La Gaceta Newspaper, Tampa, Florida, page: 48; Smithsonian American Art Museum, Washington, D.C., Hemphill/Art Resource, New York, page: 52; © Private Collection/© Christie's Images/The Bridgeman Art Library page: 56; Courtesy of Cesar Gonzalez page: 58; Courtesy of Fred Morales, El Paso/Juarez Historian page: 68; Courtesy of League of United Latin American Citizens pages: 72, 78, 84; © Private Collection/Archives Charmet/The Bridgeman Art Library page: 75; Associated Press pages: 86, 93, 95

Maps: Created by Ortelius Design

Printed in the United States of America

Bang CMA 10 9 8 7 6 5 4 3 2 1

This book is printed on acid-free paper.

Contents

Preface to the Series

**by Mark Overmyer-Velázquez, Ph.D.,
Consulting Editor**

"With all due respect to Uncle Sam, this [march] shows that Los Angeles has never stopped belonging to Mexico." This statement by Alberto Tinoco, a television reporter in Mexico, refers to the demonstration in support of immigrants that took place in Los Angeles, California, on March 25, 2006. An estimated 1 million people attended this march—mainly Mexicans and other Latinos. But does Los Angeles belong to Mexico? And what was so important that so many people came out to show their support for Latino immigrants?

The *Latino American History* series looks to answer these questions and many others. Los Angeles did belong to Mexico until 1848. At that time, Los Angeles and much of what is now called the American Southwest became part of the United States as a result of the Mexican-American War. Today, the enormous city, like many other places throughout the United States, is home to millions of Latinos.

The immigrant march made perfectly clear that people of Latin American descent have a historical power and presence in the United States. Latino history is central to

OPPOSITE In the late 1930s, a demonstration in front of the San Antonio, Texas, City Hall is directed by Latina labor leader Emma Tenayuca.

the history of the United States. Latinos have been closely connected to most regions in the United States in every era, from the 16th-century Spanish settlements in Florida and California to the contemporary surge of Latino populations in North Carolina, South Carolina, Oklahoma, Minnesota, and Connecticut.

The 2000 U.S. Census made Latinos' importance even plainer. Every 10 years, the government makes a survey of the country's population, called a census. The 2000 survey determined that, for the first time, Latinos outnumbered African Americans as the second-largest nonwhite population.

One of every seven people in the nation identifies himself or herself as Latino. This ethnic group has accounted for about half the growth in the U.S. population since 1990. There are over 41 million people of Latin American and Caribbean origins in the United States. Their presence will have a large impact on the futures of both the United States and Latin America.

Who Is Latino?

The term *Latino* emerged in the 1970s. It refers—somewhat loosely—to people, either male or female, living in the United States who have at least one parent of Latin American descent. The term is often used in contrast to terms such as *Anglo American, African American,* and *Asian American.* Most frequently, *Latino* refers to immigrants (and their descendants) who originally came to the United States from the Spanish-speaking countries of North, Central, and South America, as well as from countries in the Caribbean. This definition usually does not include Brazil, Haiti, and Belize, where the chief language is not Spanish, but does include Puerto Rico, which is a U.S. territory.

The other popular term to describe this population, *Hispanic,* was developed by the U.S. government in the 1970s as a way to categorize people of Latin American descent. However, Latinos consider this label to wrongly identify them more with Spain than with Latin America. In addition, most Latinos first identify with their own national or subnational (state, city, or village) origins. For example, a woman with roots in the Dominican Republic might first identify herself as *una dominicana* and then as a Latina. The word *Latino* causes further confusion when discussing the thousands of non–Spanish-speaking American Indians who have immigrated to the United States from Latin America.

Four main factors over time have determined the presence of Latinos in the United States. They are U.S. military and economic involvement in Latin America, relaxed immigration laws for entry into the United States, population growth in Latin America, and wages that were higher in the United States than in Latin America. These factors have shaped the patterns of migration to the United States since the mid-19th century.

"We Didn't Cross the Border, the Border Crossed Us"   1848

Many Mexicans still call the Mexican-American War from 1846 to 1848 the "North American Invasion." In the first decades of the 19th century, Mexico's economy and military were weak from years of fighting. There had been a war for independence from Spain followed by a series of civil wars among its own people. During the same period, the United States was eager to expand its borders. It looked to Mexico for new land. The war cost Mexico almost half its territory, including what would become the U.S. states of California, Nevada, Arizona, New Mexico, and Texas. Some Mexican citizens left on the U.S. side of the new border proclaimed, "We didn't cross the border, the border crossed us."

The territory that had belonged to Mexico brought new citizens of Mexican background to the United States, as well as enormous mineral and land wealth. Consider the famous gold rush that started in 1848 on former Mexican territory in California. That event and the vast expanse of farmlands and pasture lands once belonging to Mexico were vital to the westward expansion of the United States. Mexicans on the north side of the new border became U.S. citizens and the country's first Latinos. As the West became industrialized and demand for labor grew, it was often migrant Mexican workers who labored in the fields and factories of the prospering economy.

1898   The Spanish-American War, Puerto Rico, and the Harvest of Empire

The term *harvest of empire* refers to the arrival of Latino immigrants in the United States as a direct result of U.S. military involvement in Latin America, starting with Mexico in 1848. The United States created political and economic uncertainty through the use of force and the support of dictatorships in the "garden" of Latin America. Then the United States harvested the resulting millions of homeless and jobless Latinos. The United States's harvest of empire peaked with the 1898 Spanish-American War.

Fast Fact

American Indians who have migrated to the United States may identify themselves with a small village or perhaps a state of origin. For example, Zapoteco immigrants from the state of Oaxaca, Mexico, have developed Oaxacan hometown associations in Los Angeles and other U.S. cities.

The U.S. military freed the island of Puerto Rico from Spanish colonial rule in 1898. The island's residents never would have imagined that they would be colonized yet again, this time by the United States. The island became a U.S. territory. The U.S. president had the power to choose the governor and other high-level administrators. In 1917, Congress made all Puerto Ricans U.S. citizens.

In the 1950s, Puerto Rico suffered economic problems and joblessness. Immigration to the United States rapidly expanded, resulting in the largest movement of Latin Americans to the United States in history. New laws in the 1960s only increased Latin American immigration to the United States.

The Hart-Celler Act and Recent Latino Migration   1965

On October 3, 1965, President Lyndon Johnson signed the Hart-Celler Act, introducing a new era of mass immigration. The act made people's work skills and their need to unite with their families the most important elements in deciding who could immigrate to the United States. The new legislation eventually ended a system that used people's countries of origin to decide the number of immigrants who were allowed into the United States. The Hart-Celler Act supposedly put people of all nations on an equal footing to immigrate to the United States. The act created the foundation for today's immigration laws.

Between 1960 and 2000, Latin America's population skyrocketed from 218 million to over 520 million. Political instability in the region, in addition to this growing population, meant increased needs for migration and work. Many people turned to the economic opportunities of the United States as a strategy for survival.

At the same time, in the United States, agricultural, industrial, and domestic employers depended upon the ability to pay immigrant laborers from Latin America lower wages. As a result, Latino labor has almost always been welcomed in the United States, despite the government's repeated attempts to restrict immigration in the past century. The demands of U.S. employers for Latino immigrant labor have always shaped the tone of the immigration debate.

Fast Fact

In 1960, 75 percent of the foreign-born population of the United States came from Europe. Only 14 percent came from Latin America and Asia. As a result of the Hart-Celler Act, by 2000, only 15 percent of immigrants were European and more than 77 percent were Latin American and Asian. This trend promises to continue.

Many Latino Histories

The events of the years 1848, 1898, and 1965 explain how and why Latinos migrated to the United States. However, these events do not reveal much about what happened once the Latinos arrived. Despite their many shared experiences, Latinos are anything but an easily defined people. Although television and film have tended to portray all Latinos as similar, they come from a wide range of national, ethnic, social, economic, and political backgrounds, which have divided as much as united this growing population. Such backgrounds include "African," "Anglo," "Asian," "Indian," and any combinations of these.

Mexicans started migrating to the United States in the 19th century and Puerto Ricans in the early 20th century. Immigrants from Chile, Argentina, El Salvador, Guatemala, and other South and Central American countries made their way north in large numbers starting in the 1960s. Many of these Latinos were seeking shelter from brutal military dictatorships. Once in the United States, Latinos of all backgrounds have continued to mix with each other and with local populations, forging a whole new set of identities. Latino communities keep and develop their own cultures in new and creative ways in the United States, adding to the rich diversity of the country.

Indeed, Latinos have contributed to U.S. society in other ways besides their investments in the country's economy and labor. In politics, education, sports, and the arts, Latinos are a growing presence. By exploring the origins and development of U.S. Latinos, this series, *Latino American History,* helps us to better understand how our Latin American neighbors to the south have become our Latino neighbors next door.

Introduction

The history of Latinos in the United States began hundreds of years ago, when explorer Christopher Columbus discovered and claimed the West Indies for Spain in 1492. Spanish conquistadores later conquered areas of South, Central, and North America.

As the Spaniards staked out an empire in the Americas, American Indians whose ancestors had lived in the region for centuries suffered. Everywhere they went, the Spanish conquered and enslaved the native people. Diseases that the Spanish had carried with them from Europe wiped out whole populations of Indians, who had no natural resistance to these illnesses. The Spaniards also brought kidnapped men, women, and children from Africa to work in New Spain as slaves.

Spanish men outnumbered Spanish women in the new American colonies. As a result, men from Spain often had children with native or slave women. Native people often married African slaves. These three groups all played important roles in the development of a new people, the Latinos. Latino Americans today are descended from the Spanish-speaking colonists who settled in New Spain. Most are also descended from the Indian and African people who lived in the Spanish colony.

OPPOSITE The female figure in this painting represents America leading pioneers and railroads westward during the 1800s. This expansion included movement into parts of North America with large Latino populations formerly owned by Spain and Mexico.

Spain in the United States

Spain was the first European power to claim chunks of land in what is now the United States. Beginning in 1513, when Juan Ponce de León claimed Florida for Spain, the Spanish gained control of an area that included most of the southern and southwestern regions of the present-day United States.

In the 1800s, people in the Americas began to revolt against Spanish colonialism. In 1821, Spain lost control of its most important North American territory, Mexico. This included all or parts of present-day Texas, California, New Mexico, Arizona, Nevada, Utah, Colorado, and Wyoming.

Mexico, however, would not be able to hang on to its lands to the north and northwest for long. At this time, many U.S. citizens believed that the United States was entitled to rule over the entire North American continent, an idea that was known as manifest destiny. During the 1800s, people in the United States left the East Coast and began settling west of the Mississippi. In 1837, U.S. citizens in Texas revolted against Mexican control and formed their own republic. Texas became part of the United States in 1845.

After the Mexican-American War (1846–1848), all of Mexico's territory above the Rio Grande was signed over to the United States. With the stroke of a pen, people of Spanish descent in these territories became citizens of the United States.

Fast Fact

The term *manifest destiny* was coined by writer John Louis O'Sullivan in 1845. In an editorial that supported claiming Texas for the United States, O'Sullivan wrote, "Other nations have tried to check . . . the fulfillment of our manifest destiny to overspread the continent allotted by Providence for the free development of our yearly multiplying millions."

In the coming half-century, Latinos made great contributions to the prosperity and success of the United States. They worked as farmers, ranchers, and gold miners, helping the Southwest grow and develop. They also created a unique lifestyle that combined Spanish and U.S. culture. Today, the Latino influence of these early days can still be seen and felt throughout the Southwest and West.

With the Southwest in U.S. hands, Mexican immigration into the United States officially began. From that point until the present day, Mexicans have made up the largest part of Latino migration to the United States. However, in the late 1800s, as the United States became an important economic and world power, Latinos from Chile, Cuba, Puerto Rico, and other former Spanish colonies began immigrating to the United States. Most of these people were fleeing political turmoil or poverty in their native countries. Like immigrants from other parts of the world who have come to the United States throughout the centuries, these Latino people hoped to find a better life for themselves and their families.

The late 1800s also marked the beginnings of U.S. interference in Latin America. As Spain gave up its claims to former colonies, many U.S. politicians and citizens hoped to take control. U.S. politicians wanted to make sure that Spain and other European nations had no colonies in the Americas. At the same time, U.S. businesses stepped in to buy up land in former Spanish colonies, marking the start of U.S. economic control of many Caribbean islands and Latin American countries. Such political and economic interference marked the beginning of a new relationship between the United States and its neighbors to the south.

The Big Stick of the United States

1

The U.S. government first chose to become involved in Latin American affairs during the Spanish-American War (1898). The war was the result of tensions between Spain and the United States over the island of Cuba. Seventy-five years earlier, the United States had proclaimed the Monroe Doctrine. This official document stated that the United States would not tolerate European nations setting up any more colonies in the Western Hemisphere. Now, invoking the spirit of anticolonialism set forth in the Monroe Doctrine, the United States supported the efforts of Cuban freedom fighters to win their country's independence from Spain. In addition, many U.S. residents had a financial interest in Cuba, which was home to a large number of U.S. businesses.

In February 1898, the U.S. battleship *Maine* blew up in the harbor at Havana, Cuba. About 260 people were killed in the explosion. The exact cause of the blast remains a mystery to this day, although most historians believe that it was an accidental explosion inside the *Maine's* hold. U.S. officials, however, quickly blamed Spain. Outraged U.S. citizens,

OPPOSITE   President Theodore Roosevelt swings a "big stick," representing the threat of force, at "every thing in general" in this cartoon from 1904.

fueled by anti-Spanish newspaper reports, demanded that the United States strike back. In April, the two countries went to war.

Although the United States backed Cuba's freedom fighters, many U.S. residents saw the war as an opportunity to expand U.S. influence. The island, located just 90 miles (145 km) away from Key West, Florida, would be a natural extension of U.S. territory and would make the United States stronger economically and militarily.

This illustration of the destruction of the U.S. battleship *Maine* in Havana Harbor on February 15th, 1898, appeared in U.S. magazines shortly after the event.

Some U.S. politicians, however, believed that Cuba should be a free nation, under its own government. These politicians, led by Senator Henry M. Teller of Colorado, passed a law that denied the U.S. government the right to annex, or take over, Cuba after the war. The Teller Amendment, passed on April 19, 1898, by the U.S. Congress, included the following passage: "The United States hereby disclaims any disposition or intention to exercise sovereignty, jurisdiction, or control over said island except for pacification thereof, and asserts its determination, when that is accomplished, to leave the government and control of the island to its people."

The Spanish-American War lasted less than four months. After the war, Spain handed over Guam, Puerto Rico, and the Philippines to the United States. In return, Spain received $20 million. The United States would govern and control its new territories for many years to come.

Cuba was awarded its independence. However, the United States effectively controlled the country by placing U.S. military leaders at the head of Cuba's new government. In the coming years, the United States would take control of more and more of Cuba's government and economy.

Cuban freedom fighter José Martí had accurately predicted that once the United States became involved in Cuban affairs, it would want to keep control there. Martí, a writer and poet born in Cuba in 1853, fled to New York in 1880. During his 14 years in New York, he wrote about subjects that interested him: American Indian rights, terrorist attacks, labor strikes, and above all, the plight of his native Cuba. Martí organized Cubans living in the United States into a strong, vocal independence movement.

In the late 1880s and early 1890s, Martí was appointed U.S. consul to Uruguay and Argentina. There, he saw firsthand the U.S. efforts to take economic control of Latin

Life at the Turn of the Century

The United States of 1900 was very different from the United States of today. Five future states—Oklahoma, New Mexico, Arizona, Alaska, and Hawaii—had yet to be added to the nation. The United States also controlled Puerto Rico, Guam, the Philippines, and American Samoa. In 1900:

- Only 76 million people lived in the United States (compared with 300 million today)
- The average household contained seven people
- Women could vote in only four states
- As many as half of all people in the United States lived in poverty
- About 60 percent of all people in the United States lived on farms or in rural areas
- One out of every ten households had electricity
- The total number of cars registered in the country was about 8,000.

America. He quickly realized that any help from the United States would come at a high price for Cuba. In 1895, shortly before his death, Martí wrote in a letter, "It is my duty to prevent, through the independence of Cuba, the U.S.A. from spreading over the West Indies and falling with added weight upon other lands of Our America."

A Big Stick in the Western Hemisphere

As the United States became more powerful, its relationships with nearby countries began to change. In the early 1900s, the United States adopted a "big stick" policy when dealing with countries in Latin America. The name of this policy came from a saying that was often quoted by U.S. president Theodore Roosevelt: "Speak softly and carry a big stick." When politicians talked about a "big stick," they meant the threat of force that the powerful United States could use against smaller, weaker countries that threatened U.S. interests.

The official name for this big stick policy was the Roosevelt Corollary, an addition to the Monroe Doctrine. The Roosevelt Corollary stated that "chronic wrongdo-ing" in the Western Hemisphere would force the United States to get involved as an "international police force." The new policy gave the United States the freedom to involve itself in the affairs of Latin American countries. Until the late 1930s, the United States would use the Roosevelt Corollary as an excuse to get involved in the affairs of Honduras, El Salvador, Guatemala, Nicaragua, and Costa Rica.

Under President William Howard Taft, the United States developed "dollar diplomacy" to further control Latin America. With dollar diplomacy, the United States extended its control and influence throughout the region by using its financial and economic power to grant loans to poor Latin American nations and companies. These loans made Latin America even more dependent upon the United States.

The United States in Puerto Rico

After the Spanish-American War, Puerto Rico became a protectorate of the United States. A protectorate is a nation that is protected by a larger, more powerful country. Puerto Ricans had been struggling for independence from Spain since 1868. At the end of 1897, islanders had been granted self-rule by Spain under the Charter of Autonomy. Now under U.S. control, citizens of the little island, located

1,000 miles (1,600 km) southeast of Florida, had fewer rights than they had been granted in 1897.

The United States quickly set up a military government in Puerto Rico. The new government improved the island's infrastructure by building highways, repairing roads, and updating the sanitation system. Government officials also started a public school system. However, the U.S. generals in charge of the new government had little sympathy for the Puerto Ricans, and many freedoms and efforts at self-government were curbed during this period.

José Celso Barbosa was a strong advocate for Puerto Rican statehood.

After Puerto Rico became a U.S. possession, many Puerto Rican immigrants who were living in the United States returned to the island. Some, like Dr. José Celso Barbosa, became leaders in island political movements. Barbosa founded a political party that advocated statehood for Puerto Rico and also served as a senator in Puerto Rico. Until his death in 1921, he fought to win the same rights for Puerto Ricans as U.S. citizens on the mainland enjoyed. He wrote, "We want, and we ask, for equality. Not colonialism or protection. Since the American Flag first waved over Puerto Rico, those have been the ideals that we have defended." Today, Barbosa is known as the father of the Puerto Rican statehood movement. Puerto Ricans celebrate his birthday, July 27, as an official holiday.

The Foraker Act

In April 1900, the United States passed the Foraker Act, also known as the Organic Act of 1900. Under this law, the U.S. president appointed a Puerto Rican governor and an executive council to govern the island. The act also set up a 35-member legislature, elected by the people of Puerto Rico, and a judicial system. The act provided for Puerto Rico to have a voice in the U.S. Congress, although the island's representative, called a resident commissioner, was not allowed to vote. As a result, the resident commissioner was not very influential.

Most important, the people of Puerto Rico were not considered citizens of the United States, so they did not have the rights that U.S. citizens enjoyed. This state of affairs upset many islanders. Luis Muñoz Rivera, an important Puerto Rican politician, wrote an open letter to U.S. president William McKinley to protest the Foraker Act. The act, he wrote, was "unworthy of the United States which imposes it and of Puerto Ricans who have to endure it."

Luis Muñoz Rivera

Luis Muñoz Rivera (1859–1916), was a passionate supporter of Puerto Rico's independence from Spain. When the United States invaded Puerto Rico in 1898, Muñoz Rivera spoke out against U.S. interference in his land. The following year, he moved to New York, where he founded a bilingual newspaper called the *Puerto Rico Herald*. In it, he wrote, "If the United States continues to humiliate and shame us, we can forget about statehood and support independence, with or without U.S. protection."

In 1904, after returning to Puerto Rico, Muñoz Rivera founded the Unionist Party, a political party that lobbied for Puerto Rican independence and greater self-rule. In 1910, Muñoz Rivera was elected the island's resident commissioner. In this role, he lobbied Congress for greater self-government for his country. Muñoz Rivera died in 1916, one year before the United States repealed the much-hated Foraker Act.

Puerto Rico's new civil government was put into place in May 1900. Several of the chief officials of the U.S.-appointed government were from the mainland. For example, the first governor of the island was Charles H. Allen, a former congressman from Massachusetts and assistant secretary of the navy. The U.S. leaders of Puerto Rico's civil government, no matter how well intentioned they might have been, had several barriers to overcome. Language was one problem to be considered. People on the island spoke Spanish, while the new U.S. leaders spoke mainly English. In addition, Puerto Rican culture was quite different than the culture of the United States. These differences led to misunderstandings and resentment between the new governors and the islanders. Many Puerto Ricans felt that the United States was just a new colonial master, even harsher than Spain had been.

U.S. control also brought about economic changes in Puerto Rico. Absentee U.S. landowners bought up huge chunks of land on the island. They built sugar plantations and tobacco farms. In 1899, before the United States took control, Puerto Ricans owned 93 percent of all farms on their island. By 1930, U.S. businesses controlled 60 percent of the island's sugar-growing land and 80 percent of the tobacco-growing land.

Over time, the sugar industry would become the most important part of Puerto Rico's economy. In the process, subsistence farming on Puerto Rico was wiped out. Subsistence farming is the growing of food crops to feed a family or community, not to sell for profit. Instead, the sugar industry employed two out of every three Puerto

Rican workers to work *la zafra,* "the sugar harvest." However, this type of work lasted just five months of each year. For the other seven months, employment was scarce, and poverty climbed.

Puerto Rican farmers were not the only ones affected by the island's new status as a U.S. possession. Other workers throughout the country also suffered. Items like shoes, furniture, and clothing, once handcrafted in Puerto Rico by island artisans, were now manufactured in large quantities in factories in the United States and shipped to Puerto Rico. These goods quickly put the craft workers out of business.

Puerto Rican Migration

As conditions in Puerto Rico changed, many people chose to leave the island. The new ties to the United States made it easier for people to move between Puerto Rico and the mainland. Another factor was the population boom on the island. This growth in the number of people living in Puerto Rico was the result of improved health care and sanitary conditions. In the 40-year period between 1860 and 1900, the number of people in Puerto Rico nearly doubled, growing from 583,000 to 1 million. However, jobs and other economic opportunities did not increase at the same rate, so people came to the mainland to find work.

In the early years of the 20th century, migration from Puerto Rico was slow. Most of the new arrivals were young men looking for good jobs in the United States. Many of these men settled in New York City. Although most intended the move to be only temporary, some ended up staying and sending for their families. In 1910, just over 1,500 Puerto Ricans were recorded living on the mainland; two out of three lived in New York.

Early Puerto Rican immigrants to the United States were mostly uneducated and poor. They had to take unskilled, low-paying jobs, mostly in textile plants or other types of factories in the Northeast. Others, who had worked as farm laborers back home, traveled to Hawaii to try to find work on sugar plantations there. On the way to the islands in the Pacific, the migrants traveled by boat to New Orleans, Louisiana, then by train to San Francisco, California. From there, they sailed to Hawaii. Some Puerto Ricans, however, chose to remain in the two big U.S. cities that they were passing through on the way to Hawaii. As a result, small *colonias,* or communities, of Puerto Ricans were founded in both New Orleans and San Francisco.

This map of the world illustrates U.S.-controlled territories around 1900.

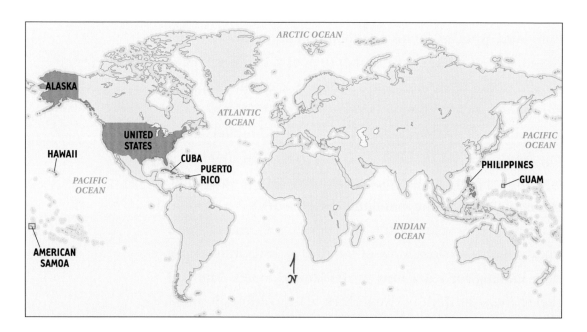

Interference and "Independence" in Cuba

In 1901, U.S. politicians again turned their attention to Cuba. That year, Congress passed the Platt Amendment. The new law allowed the United States to ignore the Teller Amendment. The Platt Amendment granted the United States the right to intervene in Cuban affairs in order to protect life, liberty, and property. It also allowed the United States to build naval bases in Cuba. Cuba was forced to include the amendment as part of its new constitution.

The Platt Amendment was applauded by U.S. business owners who wanted to protect their financial investments on the island. As in Puerto Rico, many of Cuba's businesses would soon be controlled by U.S. citizens. The United States used the Platt Amendment to send U.S. military forces to stop rebellions in Cuba in 1906 and 1912. Then, from 1917 to 1923, the U.S. military occupied the island to maintain order.

At the time of Cuban independence, the Cuban population in the United States was very small. The largest groups of Cubans were living in Key West, Tampa, and Ybor City (now a part of Miami) in Florida. Most of these earliest immigrants, whose ancestors had first arrived in the early 1830s, owned or worked in cigar-making factories. Not until the 1970s would Cubans migrate to Florida and New York in large numbers.

> **Fast Fact**
>
> The Platt Amendment was named for its sponsor, Orville Hitchcock Platt of Connecticut. Platt, one of the five most important U.S. senators in Washington during the late 1890s, also played a key role in the claiming of Hawaii and in U.S. interference in the Philippines.

Guantánamo Naval Base

In 1903, the United States began building a naval base in Guantánamo Bay in southwest Cuba. The big, deepwater bay was chosen for its important location near a shipping route that linked the Atlantic and Pacific Oceans. The naval base was built on 45 acres (18 ha) and included airfields and training grounds.

Today, Guantánamo is still controlled by the U.S. military. However, Cuba's current government resents the presence of the United States in Cuba and has, in the past, threatened to seize the base. In recent years, the base has become controversial because of its use as a detainment center for suspected terrorists from Afghanistan and Iraq. In 2006, the United Nations called for the United States to close down the base.

Now that Cuba was independent, some Cuban exiles took the opportunity to return home. Many of those who returned were political refugees who had fled to escape persecution under the Spanish government. These refugees expected to find a new, improved situation back home— and in many ways, they did. U.S. control brought improvements to public works, health care, and sanitation. Poor people were given public aid.

However, leaders who supported Cuban autonomy, or self-government, were left out of the new, U.S.-controlled government. Newspapers that dared to criticize the United States or its appointed officials in Cuba were closed down, and their editors were arrested. Cuban political leaders also charged the United States with rigging Cuba's first election so that people who supported the Platt Amendment were elected.

All Cubans suffered from racism and cultural insensitivity on the part of U.S. officials. In 1903, Leonard Wood, the military governor of Cuba, wrote to President McKinley about the Cuban efforts toward self-government: "We are going ahead as fast as we can, but we are dealing with a race that has steadily been going down for a hundred years and into which we have got to infuse new life, new principles and new methods of doing things. This is not the work of a day or of a year, but of a longer period."

Seeking a Brighter Future

2

The beginning of the 20th century was a time of hardship and turmoil for most Mexicans. The country's president, Porfirio Díaz, ruled Mexico like a dictator. During his time in power, millions of acres of land were taken from Mexico's peasants and sold to the wealthy. To encourage businesses to locate in Mexico, Díaz also gave large land grants to foreign companies, especially U.S. oil and mining companies. By 1913, there were more than 500,000 people from the United States in Mexico, and they controlled about $1 billion in investments there. At the same time, about 15 million Mexicans were living in poverty. As in Puerto Rico and Cuba, subsistence farming faded away, and people started going hungry as food prices rose.

In 1910, the peasants of Mexico rose up in revolt against Díaz's government. In its earliest days, the rebellion was led by Francisco Madero, a landowner who had unsuccessfully run for president against Díaz. Many people—especially peasants—supported Madero in his efforts to bring democracy to Mexico.

OPPOSITE Francisco Madero waves from a jeep in 1911 during the Mexican Revolution. Madero led Mexican peasants in an uprising against President Porfirio Díaz.

Led by guerrilla fighters like Emiliano Zapata in the south and Pancho Villa in the north, the revolution was long and bloody. During the course of the conflict, about 1 million people were killed. Crops and railways were destroyed, and the economy was left in shambles.

When the war started, the United States chose to remain neutral. In 1913, however, President Woodrow Wilson decided to lift an arms blockade against Mexico. This decision allowed arms to reach revolutionaries now fighting against Mexico's current president, former rebel Francisco Madero. Madero had been elected president in October 1911. In 1914, after U.S. sailors were arrested in Mexico for landing in a forbidden area, the two nations nearly went to war.

Many Mexicans were unhappy with U.S. interference in the revolution. One such person was Francisco "Pancho" Villa. In 1916, Villa began attacking U.S. citizens in Mexico and in U.S. border towns. In January, he stopped a train in Mexico and killed 15 mining engineers from the United States. Two months later, he attacked the town of Columbus, New Mexico, and killed 17 U.S. citizens. As a result of these incidents, President Wilson severed relations with Mexico and sent 6,000 troops under General John J. Pershing to capture Villa. However, the Mexican revolutionary escaped and became a hero to many Mexicans.

Some Mexicans in the United States managed to support the revolution from afar. Ricardo and

Fast Fact

In 1910, the U.S. Census counted about 500,000 Latinos living in the United States. However, more recent figures, based on an in-depth study of census data from 1910, reveal a much larger Latino-American population. The new study estimates that about 845,000 Latinos made their homes in the United States at this time.

Enrique Flores Magón were brothers who published a news-paper against Díaz's government in the early 1900s. To escape persecution, the two fled to St. Louis, Missouri, in 1905. Here, Ricardo founded a political party to oppose Díaz. In 1911, the brothers led the Magonista Revolt, an uprising of liberal rebels living in Baja California against the Díaz government.

The Mexican Revolution (1910–1920) caused a huge increase in immigration from Mexico to the United States. People of all classes—from the wealthiest to the poorest—fled the devastation caused by the bloody fighting. Some were political refugees. Others left to avoid being forced to serve in the military. The majority of the immigrants, poor peasants, were looking for jobs, food, and safety for their families.

Although the revolution ended in 1920, outbreaks of violence contin-ued through 1934. From 1910 to 1930, an estimated one out of every ten Mexicans migrated to the United States. Of these, more than 700,000 came legally, paying the four-dollar tax to enter the country. Many more—especially those too poor to afford the tax—came illegally. Only the beginning of the Great Depression in 1929 would put an end to the steady flow of immigration from Mexico.

Pancho Villa became a hero of the Mexican Revolution because of his successful raids against U.S. border towns.

Many of the new arrivals settled in Texas and California. Two Mexicans who arrived in the United States during the Mexican Revolution were the parents of future Texas congressman and Mexican rights advocate Henry B. Gonzalez. Leonides and Genoveva Gonzalez settled in San Antonio, Texas, in 1911. Leonides found work as an editor at *La Prensa,* a Spanish-language daily newspaper.

Discrimination against Latinos

Like immigrants from some European countries, Latinos were discriminated against by many U.S. citizens and U.S. society in general. At the turn of the century, Latinos earned lower wages and paid higher rents for inferior housing than U.S. citizens did. The discrimination against Latinos was especially apparent in the Southwest.

When Latinos were living under Mexican rule, they had not needed to worry about discrimination and prejudice. After the region came under U.S. control, their civil rights were eroded. After Mexico gave up the Southwest, California, and other territories to the United States in 1846, many areas passed laws that discriminated against Latinos. In some places, Latinos could not vote and were treated unfairly by the new U.S. judicial and education systems.

Even before the Mexican Revolution began, attacks by bandits, raiding, and incidents of anti–United States violence along the border and in Mexico had caused a "brown scare," or fear of Mexicans, especially in Texas and other parts of the U.S. Southwest. Violence against Mexicans became commonplace in the Southwest, where gangs beat up and even murdered Latinos. In 1912, such brutality became so widespread that Mexico's ambassador made a formal protest to the United States on behalf of Mexicans living in the United States.

The brutality caused many Mexicans to return to Mexico, despite the revolution there. In 1915, Mexican general León Caballo showed newspaper reporters letters he had been given by Latinos living in Texas. He told the reporters,

> *These . . . are from my people who cannot live any longer in the state of Texas, as . . . many have been killed by irresponsible armed posses without reason. They are afraid to live there, and are leaving small farms which they have purchased with the savings of a lifetime. Leaving everything behind, they are coming back [to Mexico].*

In this engraving from the early 1900s, Texas Rangers are shown arresting a group of Mexicans. The Rangers patrolled the U.S.–Mexican border and arrested or killed many Latinos they suspected of being outlaws.

Others, however, chose to fight against repression. In 1915, Mexicans living in South Texas planned an open war against the Anglos of the area. The so-called Plan of San Diego was to begin on February 20. Mexicans called on all Latinos, blacks, American Indians, and Japanese to rise up and wipe out all Anglo males over the age of 16. The goal of the revolt was to take control of the states of Texas, New Mexico, Arizona, California, and Colorado. These states would be formed into an independent republic, which could later be annexed by Mexico.

The plan for the revolt was discovered in January 1915, when a letter containing details was intercepted at the border. Anglos waited nervously for the planned rebellion to begin, but for many months nothing happened. Then in July, Mexicans in Texas began a series of raids. Texas officials were ready to retaliate. Between 1914 and 1919, the Texas Rangers, a group of armed men hired to police the border between Texas and Mexico, killed an estimated 5,000 Latinos.

The Mexican Revolution and the resulting increase in immigration to the United States only added to anti-Mexican sentiment among U.S. residents. After Pancho Villa's raids began in 1916, officials in El Paso, Texas, began rounding up Mexicans who were suspected of supporting Villa or being anti–United States. These people were promptly deported to Mexico. Editors of Spanish-language newspapers were also punished for publishing articles that criticized U.S. intervention in Mexico. In Los Angeles, California, officials banned the sale of guns and alcohol to Mexicans, and a special spy team was organized to keep track of Mexicans in the city.

The new Mexican immigrants faced discrimination not only from whites but also from other Latinos—those who had come to the United States decades earlier. The earlier arrivals, now well established, looked down on the new immigrants because of their poverty, illiteracy, and lack of sophistication. The new arrivals had different customs and spoke a different type of Spanish. A class system developed among Latinos, with the older group of Latinos on the top and the poorer new arrivals from southern and central Mexico on the very bottom.

Latinos at Work

Despite prejudice and discrimination, the United States needed the influx of Mexican immigrants. These new arrivals were looking for jobs. They were willing to work hard and perform the types of tedious, dangerous, or dirty jobs that many people did not want to do. After enduring unemployment or jobs that paid very low wages, the Mexican immigrants were also willing to work for far less pay than most U.S. citizens.

Men, women, and even children from Mexico found jobs in the fields and factories of the United States. Others ranched, helped build railroads, and labored in mines. Thanks to their hard labor, the economy in the region prospered. Soon, company owners in the Southwest began actively recruiting workers

Fast Fact

Mexican workers were not only paid less than Anglo workers; they were also paid less than other immigrant laborers. In 1908, the Southern Pacific Railroad paid Greek workers $1.60 per day, while Japanese workers were paid $1.50 per day. Mexican workers received $1.25 per day.

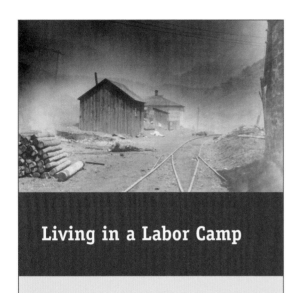

Living in a Labor Camp

In the mid-1920s, a minister described the camps that Mexican farm workers lived in.

Shelters were made of almost every conceivable thing—burlap, canvas, palm branches. Not a single wooden floor was observed in the camp. . . . There was a huge pile of manure close by the houses. . . . There were flies everywhere. . . . We found one woman carrying water in large milk pails from the irrigation ditch. The water was brown with mud, but we were assured that after it had been allowed to settle . . . it would be clear and pure. This is evidently all the water which they have in camp. There were no baths.

from Mexico. In the coming years, factory owners in the Midwest would do the same.

In the early 1900s, seven out of every ten Latino workers identified themselves as laborers (not in farming or mining). This figure included those who worked on the railroads that were being built across the country, as well as those who worked in factories. Other Latinos worked on U.S. farms. During the first decade of the 20th century, many worked in California's Imperial Valley, home of the state's cotton industry.

On farms, the Mexican family often worked as a unit, with everyone working together to plant, grow, and harvest crops. Every family member who was capable was expected to do his or her part to earn money. Despite child labor laws, farm owners often turned a blind eye to Mexican children working in the fields alongside their parents.

Farming was unskilled labor. Farm workers were expected to put in long hours, from sunup to sundown. Latinos were paid as little as one dollar a day, and the homes and food they were provided with were usually awful. Workers might live in tents or shacks with no electricity or running water. Dishonest employers sometimes cheated the workers out of their meager wages, firing them before they were paid or reporting illegal immigrants for deportation. Another trick was to withhold part of a worker's wages to pay for food, water, and other items.

Although the Mexican immigrants were performing poorly paid, unskilled labor, they were often accused of taking jobs from "real" U.S. citizens who needed work. Adding to the resentment against Mexican workers was the fact that some U.S. companies hired Mexicans as strike-breakers, workers who would cross picket lines when the regular employees went on strike. (A strike is the organized act of stopping work in order to force an employer to improve working conditions.)

Early Struggles for Equality

Many Latinos were not willing to accept unfair treatment and discrimination in the workplace. In 1903, Mexican copper miners in Clifton, Arizona, went on strike when mine owners lowered their wages but not the wages of white workers. The strike was one of the earliest copper mine strikes in the Southwest—and the first organized strike of Mexican workers in the United States. However, the strike failed. White workers refused to support the strike, and the strike's leaders were eventually arrested.

The same year, 200 Mexican and 1,000 Japanese sugar beet workers went on strike in Oxnard, California. Banding

El Congreso Mexicanista

In September 1911, Mexican Americans from across Texas met in Laredo to take part in the first Congreso Mexicanista, or Mexican Congress. The meeting attracted members of Latino societies, journalists, labor leaders, and women's leaders. For nine days, the participants discussed ways to end the violence and discrimination against Mexican Americans in the state. Both men and women attended, and at the end of the congress, two new Mexican civil rights groups were formed. One was called the *Gran Liga Mexicanista de Beneficencia y Protección* (Great Mexican League for Benefit and Protection). The second group, the *Liga Femenil Mexicanista* (Female Mexican League) was the women's branch of the group. In the coming years, members of both groups would fight for the right of Mexican-American children to attend Anglo-American schools.

together, the Latinos and Asians formed the Japanese-Mexican Labor Association, a short-lived union. The strike marked the first time that two immigrant groups worked together for better labor conditions. The strike was successful, forcing the sugar beet growers in the region to agree to the strikers' demands.

Ten years later, strikes that included Mexican workers in California and Colorado brought national attention to poor labor conditions. In 1913, Mexican and other workers at a hops farm near Wheatland, California, went on strike. The strike ended unsuccessfully with the deaths of four people after sheriffs arrived to break up a workers' meeting. However, newspaper reports about the event led to the establishment of the California Commission on Immigration and Housing, which regulated the living conditions in California farm labor camps.

In 1914, a strike of Mexican and other immigrant laborers at a mine in Ludlow, Colorado, resulted in one of the bloodiest events in U.S. labor history. On April 20, Colorado's state militia attacked the tents of workers at the Colorado Fuel & Oil Company, owned by millionaire John D. Rockefeller. The soldiers fired bullets into the crowd of striking workers, then doused the workers' tents with kerosene and set them on fire. The smoke caused the deaths of 18 people, including 13 women and children. Nine of the dead were Mexican Americans. Miners in the area retaliated, killing company guards. Eventually, the U.S. Army was called in to bring the situation under control.

In the coming years, Latinos would attempt to win better work conditions with varying degrees of success. In 1915, the Chicano, or Mexican-American, copper miners in Arizona tried again. With the support of white miners, Mexicans were able to stay out on strike for five months. Mine owners finally agreed to pay them the same wages as white miners. However, more strikes failed than succeeded. Striking Latino workers faced violence from employers and other workers and deportation by government officials. ▣

Settling in a New Land

3

Most Mexicans who fled to the United States during the Mexican Revolution believed that their stay would be temporary. Once the fighting was over and conditions improved, they intended to return home. However, after the Revolution was over, the majority of Mexican immigrants chose to remain in the United States.

Most of the new arrivals maintained strong ties to their homeland. The proximity of the Mexican border made it easy for immigrants to cross and recross the Rio Grande. Said one Mexican worker, "The Mexican immigrant . . . goes and returns easily by the rails which unite the two countries without any geographical break." Unlike immigrants who traveled to the United States from Europe or Asia, Mexican immigrants had easy access to their friends and relatives back home. In Mexico they could shop, visit, absorb Mexican culture, and speak their native language. As a result, the Latino population in the Southwest was able to hold on to its language and traditions longer than immigrants to the United States from other countries.

OPPOSITE This hand-colored woodcut shows a group of Latino cowboys called *vaqueros* outside Mission Santa Inez in California during the late 1800s.

However, Mexican immigrants, like other immigrants at this time, were expected to adapt to life in the United States. They were expected to become "American." To federal, state, and local officials, this meant learning English and accepting U.S. customs and habits.

How well a Mexican immigrant adapted to life in the United States depended upon several factors. An immigrant's economic situation was one factor. Family and community support was another. For example, immigrants who joined family members already living in the United States were likely to adapt more quickly. Even the area that an immigrant came from made a difference. For example, those from northern Mexico were more likely to have been exposed to the Anglo-Southwest culture. Those from southern Mexico, farther away from the border, had a harder time adapting. By 1900, many of the new immigrants to the United States were coming from this area.

One institution that helped Latinos assimilate, or fit in, to U.S. culture was the Roman Catholic Church. Most Latino immigrants were Catholic, and the church helped the new arrivals assimilate by providing

Santeria

Some immigrants from Cuba and Puerto Rico practiced Santeria, a religion that combined West African and Catholic beliefs. Santeria originated among Cuban slaves, who combined the religious customs of their native countries in Africa with the Catholic practices of the Spanish conquerors. Over time, the religion spread throughout the Caribbean. Those who follow Santeria worship nature gods, called orishas. In the early days of slavery in Cuba, slaves disguised their worship of these nature gods by linking each god with a Catholic saint. For example, the war god Ogun was worshipped as Saint Peter. The chief god in Santeria is Olorun. Followers of Santeria choose a patron spirit to which they pray.

citizenship classes, English instruction, private schools, and youth activities.

Latino children were usually the main targets of assimilation efforts. In the early 1900s, there were more opportunities than in previous years for Latino children to attend U.S. schools. However, the number of Latino children attending school, especially in the Southwest, was still very low. In 1900, just under half of all Latino children between the ages of five and 17 in New Mexico were enrolled in public schools. In Texas, the number was much lower: less than one out of five Latino children of school age were enrolled in schools.

Part of the problem was the low value that some Latino parents placed on education. Some parents understood that an education was an important tool to help their children advance in society. Others, however, needed the income their children brought in when they worked. Still other parents worried that public education was weakening their children's link to their Latino culture.

Latino children who did attend school most often received a poor education—one that was inferior to the education received by most Anglo students. Latino children attended segregated, or separate, schools that focused less on academics than on assimilation and life skills. These segregated schools were not equal to those for other children. The buildings were often rundown, with little play space and second-rate equipment. Communities were not willing to spend the money needed to improve schools for Latino children. The teachers at these schools were often new teachers or teachers who had performed poorly at

Anglo schools. Some teachers were not able to speak Spanish—a problem when trying to communicate with immigrant children.

Mexican-American Communities in the Early 1900s

Many villages in Mexico and the U.S. Southwest resembled the pueblo in this painting.

Mexican immigrants looking for work settled in colonias, colonies of Mexican workers. In agricultural areas, these colonias started off as farming or tent communities. In Texas, many towns were founded in cotton-growing areas, while towns in California and Colorado were founded in sugar beet areas. In Arizona and New Mexico, colonias were founded near mines. Along the railroad lines, workers started colonias in old boxcars. These communities of immigrants attracted both Mexicans and Anglos.

In the cities, Mexican immigrants settled together in barrios, or neighborhoods. Like other immigrant neighborhoods in big cities across the United States, most barrios were located in the worst parts of the cities. As more immigrants arrived from Mexico, the neighborhoods filled to capacity. Cheaply built houses were put up for the new arrivals. New barrios grew up alongside the old ones. As the barrios grew in size, Latino entrepreneurs opened stores, restaurants, barbershops, and other businesses that catered to Latinos.

In some cities, Latinos were kept in the barrios by laws that prevented them from moving into Anglo neighborhoods. However, other immigrants preferred to live in a barrio, side by side with people who shared their culture and spoke their language.

Whether in a colonia or barrio, the family was the center of Mexican culture. The Latino family was an extended one, including parents, children, aunts, uncles, grandparents, and cousins. It also included godparents, or compadres. Because of the importance of the family unit, when one member moved, others tended to follow in order to keep the family intact.

In the United States, social functions were an important part of Latino life. Both Mexican and U.S. holidays were celebrated. Two of the most important holidays for Mexican Americans were Mexican Independence Day on September 16 and Cinco de Mayo on May 5. Cinco de Mayo commemorates the victory of Mexican forces over French troops on May 5, 1862. Such holidays allowed the Latinos to hold on to and celebrate their culture.

The Mutualista

To help each other, Mexicans and other Latino groups set up mutual aid, or self-help societies. These *mutualistas* were important to Latino communities. They offered health and life insurance, death benefits, and financial aid in times of trouble. They also offered legal services and emergency loans and even helped settle disputes between members.

The mutualistas often had their own halls—places where members could gather and socialize with other Latinos. During the early 20th century, plays, dances, meetings, and many other activities were held there. By providing community gathering spots, the mutualistas helped preserve Latino culture. Some of the mutual-aid societies even founded libraries and *escuelitas,* or "little schools," which supplemented the second-rate education received by many Latino children at this time.

Mexican mutualistas were often created by people of the same social class, usually from the same town or region in Mexico. Some groups only accepted as members those who had become U.S. citizens. Some were for men only, while others formed separate women's chapters.

At the turn of the century, one of the largest and most important of the Latino mutualistas was *La Alianza Hispano-Americana,* or the Hispanic-American Alliance. Founded in Tucson, Arizona, in 1894, the group expanded in the 1910s throughout Texas and the Southwest. At its height, the alliance included about 20,000 members throughout the Southwest. Initially, only male Mexican Americans (not of African or Asian descent) were able to join. In 1913, the group began allowing women into its ranks. The group continued to operate until the mid-1960s.

Some of the mutualistas evolved into advocacy groups that lobbied for fairer treatment of Latinos in the United States. These groups became politically active, supporting local and state politicians who were sympathetic to Latinos.

Some groups became involved in labor issues by supporting Latinos who were on strike. Other groups were founded for the purpose of preserving Latino culture.

This "reader" in a cigar factory in Tampa, Florida, in 1909 read books and newspapers at the top of his voice all day long. He was paid by the workers, who selected what he would read.

News in the Latino Community

In the early 1900s, Latinos in the Southwest began publishing newspapers to serve the region's increasing Spanish-speaking population. Most Anglo newspapers of the time contained little, mostly negative news about Mexico, Mexicans, and other Latinos. Spanish-language newspapers presented a more positive image of the Latino community in the United States.

Two of the most successful newspapers were *La Prensa,* founded in San Antonio in 1913, and *La Opinión,* founded in Los Angeles in 1926. Both papers were founded by Ignacio E. Lozano, a Mexican who had immigrated to San

Antonio in 1908. Lozano hired talented authors from Mexico, Spain, and Latin America to write articles for his newspapers. *La Prensa,* published in the Southwest, provided news about the Mexican Revolution and promoted pride in Mexico and Mexican culture. The publication also addressed issues that were important to Latinos, such as segregation and U.S. foreign policy concerning Latin America.

Fast Fact

The first Spanish-language paper in the United States, *El Misisipí,* was founded in New Orleans in 1808. This paper, published twice a week, had English translations of many articles, and the advertising was nearly all in English. It served as a guide for traders and merchants in the area.

One of sections that readers looked forward to reading in the newspapers was *la crónica,* or the chronicle. This short column poked fun at immigrants and Latinos who tried to shed their Spanish culture and become "American." In the Southwest, Mexican-American writers mocked women who cut their hair short, smoked cigarettes, or celebrated U.S. holidays like Thanksgiving. In the Northeast, Cuban, Spanish, and Puerto Rican newspaper writers had similar aims. Authors of these pieces took pseudonyms, or false names, such as the Spoiled Brat, Rattler, Aztec, and the Whip. La crónica was so popular among readers that some newspapers were entirely made up of these essays.

Although dozens of newspapers were founded during the early 20th century, most did not last. In fact, only a small number founded in the 1920s and 1930s still exist today. The oldest is *El Tiempo de Laredo,* which has been published continuously since 1926. Another surviving paper is *El Heraldo de Brownsville,* founded in Texas in 1934. Both began as Spanish editions of existing Anglo newspapers.

The early 1900s also saw the start of Spanish-language publishing houses in San Antonio, Los Angeles, and San Diego. The largest was San Antonio's Casa Editorial Lozano, founded by Ignacio Lozano. The publishing house's specialty was fictional pieces about the Mexican Revolution. Some were published first as serials in Lozano's newspapers.

One of the most famous works published by Casa Editorial Lozano was *Los de abajo,* or *The Underdogs,* by Mariano Azuela. The book, today considered a classic, depicts the destruction caused by the Mexican Revolution. Lozano also published humorous books that showed Mexican immigrants trying to adjust to life in the United States.

Latino Culture in the United States

4

atinos made important contributions to arts and entertainment in the United States. Latino music and theater of the early 20th century left a lasting impression on U.S. artists.

Music has always been an important part of Latino culture. In the early 1900s, a Mexican-American celebration was not complete without musicians. *Orquestas* played at weddings, birthday parties, parades, and other public events. The earliest orquestas centered on at least one violin. If there were other musicians around, they joined in.

By the 1920s, more formally organized orchestras were founded in Texas. Bands varied in size from four to 20 musicians, all wearing traditional cowboy outfits. Like earlier orquestas, these *orquestas típicas* played for all occasions. They were especially popular on Mexican holidays. In the 1930s, the orquesta developed into a kind of dance band that played both Latino and Anglo songs, including big band and swing music.

OPPOSITE At Latino social clubs, such as this Cuban club, Latino cultural traditions like parades and festivals were kept alive and appreciation for Latino art and music were passed down.

One style of music that was unique to Mexicans living in the Southwest was the *corrido,* or ballad. This style of song developed in Texas in the mid-1800s. Many of the corridos featured stories about Latino heroes who struggled against hatred in the United States. One, "El corrido de Gregorio Cortez," was made into a book and then into a film. The song describes a Mexican in Texas who kills a sheriff in self-defense.

In the 1920s, a hybrid called the *canción-corrido* developed. This type of song was a snapshot of Latino life in the Southwest. It included both sadness and humor. The writers and singers of these songs, known as troubadours, became famous throughout the region.

Yet another type of Latino music that developed in the Southwest was *música norteña,* also called *conjunto* by Mexicans in Texas. Conjunto musicians adopted a type of accordion from German or other European immigrants to create folk music. Later, a guitar was added. By the 1930s, conjunto was the preferred music of rural, working-class Latinos in the Southwest.

Music was important to Puerto Rican immigrants as well. Trios of

A Canción-Corrido

An excerpt from *"El lavaplatos"* ("The Dishwasher")

One day very desperate,
Because of so much revolution,
I came over to this side
[of the border]
Without paying the immigration.
Oh, what a fast one,
Oh, what a fast one,
I crossed without paying anything.
On arriving at the station,
I ran into a friend,
Who gave me an invitation
To work on el traque.
I supposed el traque
Would be some kind of warehouse,
But it was to repair the track
Where the train ran.
Oh, what a friend,
Oh, what a friend.

musicians—two guitarists and a maraca player—often played at baptisms, weddings, and other family and community gatherings. Two styles of Puerto Rican music, the *bomba* and the *plena*, influenced modern Latino music. Both styles developed from the music made by African slaves and peasants working on the sugar plantations of coastal Puerto Rico. Cuban music of the early 1900s that has influenced modern sounds includes the *dazón, rumba, son, mambo,* and *cha-cha.*

Around 1926, big U.S. record labels like Columbia and RCA began recording Latino music. Record producers traveled to Dallas, San Antonio, and Los Angeles, and rented hotel rooms where they recorded the music of Mexican-American artists onto wax disks. Copies were then made and sold throughout the nation. Today, many of these early recordings still survive.

The wax record had a major impact on the Latino farm workers and miners of the Southwest. As long as one person had a phonograph, everyone could listen to the latest records. As a result, store owners almost always kept records and phonographs in stock.

Latino Arts

The Latino artists of the early 1900s were influenced by Mexican folk and religious art. Many of these sculptors and painters traveled from town to town, searching for work. Many worked in northern New Mexico. One such artist was José Benito Ortega. Ortega was a *santero,* an artist who carved wooden figures of saints (called santos) and people.

He then finished a figure by painting it with bright colors. Like other traveling artists, Ortega would remain in one town for as long as it took him to complete his work.

This style of folk art became less popular in New Mexico after World War I (1914–1918). However, other types of artistic expression, such as backyard shrines and home altars, were brought to the region by new immigrants from Mexico. These types of artists were called *altaristas,* or altar makers.

In the 1920s, Santa Fe and Taos in New Mexico became centers for Mexican-style furniture and sculptures created for collectors and tourists. Sometimes, families worked together to produce them. One of the most important artists in this region was José Dolores López. López created unpainted wooden sculptures of saints and biblical figures. He also made such functional items as furniture, window frames, coffins, and grave markers. López's son and granddaughter carried on his artistic tradition.

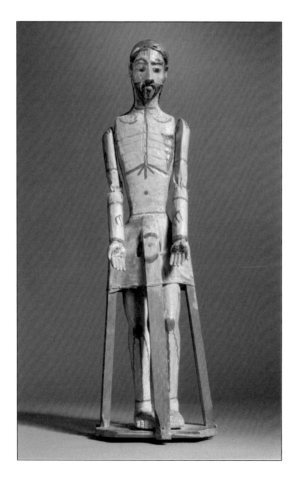

This 1885 sculpture by José Benito Ortega, called *Our Father Jesus of Nazareth,* is made of wood, cloth, leather, and metal.

Theater

Another art form that Mexican immigrants brought with them to the U.S. Southwest was theater. During the Mexican Revolution, many actors and performers fled to the United States, where they continued their careers.

The two centers of Spanish immigration, San Antonio and Los Angeles, became the centers of Latino theater in the United States. Latino theater companies from these cities and other places in the Southwest traveled as far as Tampa and New York City to play. By the 1920s, several important Latino theater companies had taken root in the United States.

As the number of Mexicans living in the United States grew in the early 1900s, touring companies from Mexico began making stops in Texas, Arizona, New Mexico, and California. Railway and automobile transportation made such tours easy and practical. To give the touring companies a place to perform, many Latino communities built their own theaters and halls. Over time, some of the Latino theaters founded their own acting companies.

The Latino theater companies were interested in promoting the work of Latino authors. Some companies commissioned works from these writers; others held contests, complete with cash prizes, for good Latino plays. Many of the works chosen for production described conditions in Mexico or the problems faced by immigrants from Mexico. Like other types of Latino literature at this time, these plays encouraged Mexicans to hold onto their heritage, to resist becoming assimilated into U.S. culture.

Other types of Latino theater that were popular in the early 1900s were vaudeville, *revistas,* or revues, and *carpas,* or tent shows. Vaudeville and revistas included singing, dancing, jokes, and some political commentary. The revista also featured Mexican customs, music, and folklore. Tent shows were often family acts that featured circus-like feats of acrobatics and daring. Carpas also included magic shows, comedy, and song-and-dance routines. One of the best-known carpas was the Carpa García. This tent show was founded by Manuel V. García, who came to the United States from Mexico in 1914. Some of the García family went on to perform with famous U.S. circuses, including Barnum and Bailey and Ringling Brothers.

Latino theater in New York was not as strong as it was in the Southwest. At the turn of the century, there were no buildings dedicated to Latino theater in New York. Instead, Latino producers rented city theaters whenever they were available. Most of the Latino actors and playwrights who were active in New York during the 1920s and 1930s were Cuban or Spanish. The most popular type of performance was *obra bufa cubana,* or the Cuban blackface farce. Characters painted their faces black, sang, danced, and performed comedy routines. Some Latino actors used the genre to attack racism.

In Tampa, with its population of Cuban tobacco workers, most shows were sponsored by the Cuban mutualistas. Many of the Tampa mutual-aid societies had their own theaters and acting companies. The

Manuel Aparicio

One of the greatest Latino actors of his time was Manuel Aparicio (birth and death dates unknown). Aparicio began his career as a cigar roller, then as a reader in a cigar factory. In the 1920s and 1930s, he became an actor and director in both Tampa and New York. During the Great Depression, Aparicio made history by directing a federal Hispanic theater company that had been established by the U.S. government. The company put on 15 different plays at the Centro Asturiano. In 1937, Aparicio and 25 Latino actors lost their jobs with the company when Congress passed a bill that prohibited giving noncitizens government work.

Cuban tobacco workers were not content with just comedies.

Tampa had several important theaters in the early 1900s. One was the Centro Asturiano, built in 1902. This 1,200-seat building hosted not only Latino productions, but also opera companies from New York and Italy. Another major theater was at the Centro Obrero, the headquarters for the Union of Tampa Cigarmakers.

Fast Fact

Many tobacco factories hired readers to come in and read books and newspapers out loud to the workers while they rolled cigars. These readings were known as *la lectura*. Some of these readers later went on to successful careers in the theater and movies.

Latino Sports

In the early 1900s, Latinos in the United States helped to develop rodeo, a sport with Mexican origins. At the same time, they left a mark on the U.S. sport of baseball. Latinos of the early 20th century also made a name for themselves in the field of professional boxing.

Rodeo, today considered a professional sport, developed from the ranching and horse-riding skills of the Latino cowboys, called *charros* in Mexico and vaqueros in the U.S. Southwest. (The English word *buckaroo* comes from Anglo attempts at pronouncing the Spanish *vaquero*). These Latino cowboys had their own dress, customs, music, and style of horsemanship. In Mexico, they held *charrerías*, or contests, which became Mexico's national sport.

Charrerías were also held at fiestas, fairs, and the large ranches in the Southwest. Cowboys competed to see who was best at riding, racing, roping, and *correr el gallo*. In this

The vaquero in this portrait from the late 1880s is wearing traditional dress—leather chaps to protect his legs, a broad-brimmed hat, and a serape over his shoulder.

event, cowboys tried to snatch a small item off the ground while riding their horses at full gallop. People traveled for miles to witness these exciting and dangerous contests. The charrerías were the forerunners of the U.S. rodeo.

The best vaqueros were hired to perform in the Wild West shows that toured the nation from the 1880s through the early 1900s. Showman Buffalo Bill Cody employed many Mexican and Mexican-American vaqueros. The most famous was Vicente Oropeza, a native of Mexico. In 1900, he became the first cowboy to win the World Championship of Trick and Fancy Roping. In 1922, he won the first World Championship Cowboy Contest in New York's Madison Square Garden. Oropeza was inducted into the Rodeo Hall of Fame in 1975.

Baseball was another sport in which Latinos excelled. This popular U.S. pastime was introduced to Cuba and other Latin American countries in the late 1800s, when U.S. baseball teams started traveling south for the winter, looking for warm places to practice. In 1878, Cuba founded its first professional baseball league—just seven years after the National Baseball Association was founded in the United States.

Before long, the Latino leagues had become a place for major league players to train. Warm Latin American countries served as winter and spring training grounds. These countries also became the permanent homes for black baseball players. At this time in the United States, blacks and whites could not play together on the same teams. Instead, blacks played on black-only teams in the Negro Leagues.

The segregation also affected Latinos baseball players. Only those with light skin who could pass as white were allowed to play in the major leagues in the United States. Those with darker skin played in the Negro Leagues or in Cuba, Mexico, or Venezuela. In all, about 50 Latino ballplayers played in the major leagues before 1947, when Jackie Robinson became the first black player. One player, Martín Dihigo, was later inducted into the Baseball Hall of Fame.

Most of the Latinos who played in the National Baseball Association played for teams in Washington, D.C.; Cincinnati or Cleveland, Ohio;

Latino Fighting Spirit

In the mid-1930s, many Puerto Ricans followed the career of boxer Sixto Escobar, *El Gallito de Barceloneta,* or "the Barceloneta Fighting Cock." Escobar, born in Barceloneta, Puerto Rico, in 1913, began his professional boxing career in 1931. He was the first Puerto Rican boxer to win a world title, in 1934. In 64 fights, he was never knocked out. Puerto Ricans were so proud of his accomplishments they named a sports stadium after him.

Another Latino fighter who was famous throughout the 1930s was Eligio "Kid Chocolate" Sardiñas. Sardiñas was born in Havana in 1910. He started fighting when he was a boy selling newspapers, to protect his turf. Sardiñas was one of the best fighters in Cuba and the United States. During his career, he won 131 bouts, including 51 knockouts. He lost just nine fights. Sardiñas was inducted into the International Boxing Hall of Fame in 1994.

Two Latino Baseball Stars

Racism made it impossible for outstanding talents like José Méndez and Martín Dihigo to get the attention and acclaim they deserved. Méndez, born in Cuba, began pitching in the U.S. Negro Leagues in 1908. During one season, he won 44 games and lost only two. Later, Méndez served as player-manager for the Kansas City Monarchs, leading them to three straight Negro National League titles from 1923 to 1925. He is currently a candidate for the Baseball Hall of Fame.

Born in Cuba in 1905, Martín Dihigo (shown above) began his career in the U.S. Negro Leagues when he was just 15 years old. By the age of 18, he was one of the top pitchers in black baseball. Dihigo also played every other position. Nicknamed "El Maestro," Dihigo was considered by some to be the best all-around baseball player who ever lived. In 1977, he was inducted into the Baseball Hall of Fame. He has also been named to the Baseball Hall of Fame in Cuba, Mexico, and Venezuela.

Chicago, Illinois; and Detroit, Michigan. Some of the teams faced public criticism for hiring players whose skin was not considered white enough.

Latinos who did play for the major leagues did not have an easy time. They were given lower pay and often faced harassment and discrimination from other players, fans, and sportswriters, both on and off the field. Light-skinned Adolfo "Dolf" Luque, who pitched for the Boston Braves, was taunted by fans whenever he took the field. Luque, nicknamed "the Pride of Havana," later played for other teams in the majors and pitched in two World Series. In 1923, he led the league with 27 wins, six shutouts, and an earned run average (ERA) of 1.93. He retired in 1935 with a career ERA of 3.24.

Latinos in the Movies

Los Angeles, because of its proximity to Hollywood, the U.S. movie capital, attracted Latinos from around the nation. During the first part of the 20th century, many Latinos found their fame and fortune there. Yet for Latinos in entertainment, such success often came with a high price.

In Hollywood, Latino actors were often assigned parts that showed how U.S. residents stereotyped all Latino people. According to one writer, "the Hispanic was one to be killed, mocked, punished, seduced, or redeemed by Anglo protagonists." On screen, the only good Latino was one of pure Spanish blood, not mixed blood, and certainly not Mexican.

As westerns became popular in the 1910s, stereotypes of the gun-toting Mexican bandito were seen across the nation. These characters were portrayed as cruel, violent, and driven by revenge. Other Latino stereotypes included the buffoon, or clown; the dark and handsome Latin lover; and the dangerous dark lady who tried—unsuccessfully— to steal the star away from his fair-skinned sweetheart.

One of the most successful male movie stars of the time was Ramón Novarro, who played the romantic lead man in many silent movies. Novarro was second in popularity only to famed silent actor Rudolf Valentino. The handsome Novarro was born in Durango, Mexico, in 1899, but Hollywood publicity agents were quick to tell fans that both his parents had come from Spain (which was not true).

One of the most famous Latino actresses to emerge at this time was Margarita Carmen Cansino, who rose to stardom as Rita Hayworth. Hayworth, whose father was Spanish, was born in Brooklyn, New York, in 1918. She began her career dancing at Mexican nightclubs, where she was spotted by a Hollywood executive while she was still a teenager. In 1937, she took the name Rita Hayworth, and her dancing, acting, and good looks—along with a hair-color change from black to auburn—turned her into a major star by the early 1940s.

> **Fast Fact**
>
> In the early 20th century, Puerto Rico had its own film industry. In 1917, writers there organized the Tropical Film Company. The company went out of business during World War I. In 1919, the Puerto Rican Photoplays Company produced a movie called *Amor tropical,* or *Tropical Love,* with U.S. actors. Unfortunately, the movie bombed, and the company went bankrupt.

While Hollywood filmmakers cranked out films filled with Latino stereotypes, Juan Emilio Viguié Cajas created his own, independent films in Puerto Rico. Most of the earliest films he made were newsreels and documentaries for U.S. companies. He covered the flights of Charles Lindbergh, the famous aviator who made the world's first solo nonstop flight across the Atlantic Ocean in 1927. Cajas made movies about Puerto Rico's government and tobacco industries. In 1934, he made his first and only feature film, a movie called *Tropical Romance.* The film was not successful, and its failure marked the end of the Puerto Rican movie industry until 1949.

The War to End All Wars

5

The Mexican Revolution was not the only violent war raging in the world during the early 1900s. In 1914, World War I broke out in Europe. The Great War pitted the Allied Powers—Great Britain, France, Russia, and Serbia—against the Central Powers—Germany, Austria-Hungary, the Ottoman Empire (present-day Turkey), and Bulgaria. For the first three years of the war, the United States remained neutral. In April 1917, however, the United States entered the conflict on the side of the Allies.

Part of the reason the United States entered the war against the Central Powers was a telegram that came to be known as the Zimmerman note. The coded telegram, sent by German foreign minister Arthur Zimmerman to the German ambassador in Mexico proposed a German-Mexican alliance against the United States. The telegram read, "We shall make war together and together make peace. We shall give general financial support, and it is understood that Mexico is to reconquer the lost territory in New Mexico, Texas, and Arizona. The details are left to you for settlement."

OPPOSITE This photograph from the early 1900s shows the first company of native Puerto Rican soldiers who enlisted in the U.S. Army. Many Latinos served in the U.S. Army during World War I.

Wilson and the Literacy Test

In 1917, President Woodrow Wilson was outraged when Congress enacted a literacy test for immigrants. Wilson had vetoed the literacy requirement twice, but Congress passed the bill over his objections. Wilson said,

In this bill it is proposed to turn away from tests of character and of quality and impose tests which exclude and restrict; for the new tests here embodied are not tests of quality or of character or of personal fitness, but tests of opportunity. Those who come seeking opportunity are not to be admitted unless they have already had one of the chief of the opportunities they seek, the opportunity of education. The object of such provision is restriction, not selection.

When the German telegram was published in U.S. newspapers, citizens were outraged. The Zimmerman note caused some to suspect that many Mexican-Americans supported Germany and the other Central Powers in the war. Latinos continued to be the target of prejudice and harassment by many U.S. citizens.

The Newest U.S. Citizens

On March 2, 1917, President Wilson signed the Jones Act into law. The law gave Puerto Ricans the option of accepting or refusing U.S. citizenship. Most became U.S. citizens.

As U.S. citizens, Puerto Ricans could come and go between the mainland and their island without a visa or any other restrictions. Yet they were not given the full rights and obligations of U.S. citizens on the mainland. For example, they were exempt from federal income tax and could not vote in national elections. They could, however, be drafted into the U.S. military. During World War I, almost 20,000 Puerto Rican soldiers took part in the conflict, and thousands died.

This cartoon appeared in the political magazine *Puck* in 1916. In it, Uncle Sam stands behind a high wall marked "Literacy Test" which is spiked with pen points. He says to an immigrant family below, "You're welcome in — if you can climb it!"

Although Puerto Ricans who had hoped for independence were not happy with the Jones Act, it was an improvement over the Foraker Act. The new law gave Puerto Rico a greater measure of self-government, including a bicameral legislature (one with two separate houses) and a bill of rights.

With movement between the island and the mainland now much easier, many poor Puerto Ricans moved to the United States looking for employment and economic opportunity. Most chose New York as a destination. Those who arrived first wrote home, telling others about available jobs and encouraging them to emigrate. Between 1898 and 1940, the number of people from Puerto Rico in New York City grew to more than 61,000.

In New York, many made their homes in Brooklyn, near the Brooklyn Navy Yard. Thousands of workers were needed there for the wartime production of battleships. During World War I, the number of workers employed at the navy yard tripled, jumping from 6,000 to 18,000.

Fighting for Democracy

In May 1917, the Selective Service Act, or draft, went into effect in the United States. The act immediately caused an uproar in the Latino community. Noncitizen Mexican men between the ages of 21 and 31 living in the United States had to register with a local draft board, even though, as Mexican citizens, they were not eligible to be drafted. Some immigrants who were unable to show a birth certificate proving they were Mexican citizens were, in fact, drafted.

Although some Latino Americans were reluctant to fight for a country that discriminated against them and treated them as inferior, others enlisted in the U.S. military. These men wanted to prove their patriotism to the United States. In fact, men of Mexican origin volunteered at a higher rate than any other ethnic group. In New Mexico, Latinos accounted for 65 percent of all those who volunteered or were drafted from the state.

Even though they were risking their lives in the war, Latino soldiers suffered discrimination in the U.S. military. They were given the worst jobs and assignments and were often ridiculed by the other U.S. soldiers. Dark-skinned men from Puerto Rico were never integrated into the army. Instead, they were sent, in segregated units, to guard the Panama Canal. Latinos who could not speak English were not integrated, either; instead, they were sent to special training centers to learn the language and train as soldiers. By the time these centers were set up, however, the war was over.

Although exact statistics on the number of Latinos who fought in World War I do not exist, it is known that thousands served with distinction. One of the many brave Latino soldiers was David Bennes Barkley, the first Latino American to be awarded the Medal of Honor. Born in Laredo, Texas, around 1899, Barkley enlisted as a private in the U.S. Army when he was 18 years old. He may have hidden his Mexican ancestry for fear of not seeing action in Europe. Barkley was sent to France with the 356th Infantry.

In France, Barkley volunteered to swim across a river between France and Germany in order to gather enemy intelligence. Although he succeeded in getting the information, he drowned on the way back. Barkley died just two days before the war ended. Barkley, whose Latino ancestry was not revealed for more than 70 years after his death, was awarded medals by France and Italy.

Nicholas Lucerno from Albuquerque, New Mexico, was awarded a French military honor called the Croix de Guerre for destroying two German machine guns. Marcelino Serna, another Latino war hero, was a Mexican immigrant

This photograph of Marcelino Serna shows him wearing his army uniform with many of his military medals.

living in El Paso when the war began. He volunteered to fight and was sent to France, where he captured 24 Germans and then protected them when another U.S. soldier wanted to kill them. He was awarded at least seven military honors, making him the most highly decorated World War I veteran in Texas.

Wartime Workers

World War I caused a boom in the U.S. economy. The United States was a main supplier of weapons and other supplies to the Allied nations in Europe. Now, with more than 2 million U.S. soldiers fighting overseas, replacement workers needed to be found. U.S. businesses looked to Mexicans and other Latinos to fill the void.

Many Mexicans, especially newly arrived immigrants, left the Southwest to find factory jobs in war-related industries, including jobs at U.S. oil fields, weapons factories, and food processing plants. They labored in Detroit automobile factories, in the meatpacking plants of Chicago, and the steel mills in Indiana, Ohio, and Pennsylvania. By 1930, 15 percent of Mexican-born U.S. residents lived outside of the traditional areas of migration.

The United States also needed more farm workers. Demand for U.S. food supplies had grown in both Europe and the United States during the war. In Europe, war had ravaged food crops. In the United States, more people were moving into city areas so the number of people growing their own food was decreasing. New advances in commercial farming now allowed previously arid land in the United States to be cultivated. Refrigerated railway cars allowed fresh vegetables and meats to be shipped across the nation.

Business owners looked for employees who would work long hours for very low wages. Latino laborers fit the bill exactly. Because they were not protected by U.S. laws and labor unions, Mexican workers could be paid half as much as Anglo workers doing the same job.

Employers looking for cheap labor faced some legal obstacles, however. In February 1917, before the U.S. had entered the war, Congress passed an immigration act meant to prevent poor and illiterate people from coming into the United States. The act required all immigrants to read and write at least one language and doubled the existing tax on their entry from four dollars to eight. The law was aimed at immigrants from southern and eastern Europe, but it affected immigration from Mexico as well. Many of the Mexican immigrants at this time were illiterate, and most were too poor to pay the new tax.

The act prompted many Mexicans looking for work to enter the country illegally. Employers were not worried about hiring illegal immigrants. In fact, they often hired Mexican-American labor contractors called *enganchistas* to find workers and transport them illegally across the border.

Smuggling Mexicans across the border illegally became a lucrative business. Smugglers were paid a fee by either the Mexicans crossing the border or the company looking for

Many Mexican immigrants found work in factories during World War I, like these women welding bomb casings in a munitions factory in 1917.

cheap labor. The first smugglers brought Mexican workers into the country by ferrying them across the Rio Grande.

In June, as labor shortages worsened, Congress waived the new criteria for Mexicans who were coming into the United States to work in agriculture. However, many employers still preferred to avoid paperwork and other requirements by hiring workers who came illegally. After the war, these illegal immigrants were the first ones to be rounded up and deported back to Mexico.

The War Ends

Despite the courageous conduct of Latino soldiers and the important work being performed by Latino laborers, the patriotism of people of Spanish ancestry was constantly questioned during the war.

In Texas, Mexican-American farmers tried to prove their patriotism and commitment to the United States by pledging to grow more food for the war effort. Spanish-language newspapers in the state tried to show Mexican-American loyalty by listing wounded and killed Mexican-American soldiers each week. Other Latino Americans showed their patriotism by buying U.S. war bonds or donating money.

When the war ended in November 1918, Latino soldiers returned from Europe wanting the same rights that they had fought to preserve. Latino veterans joined such political organizations as the American Legion and founded their own veterans' groups. Mexican veterans, for example, founded the Sons of America (SOA). The SOA encouraged Mexican immigrants to become U.S. citizens. It also fought for fair and equal treatment for all Mexican Americans. Its goal was to use "influence in all fields of social, economic, and political action in order to realize the greatest enjoyment possible of all the rights and privileges . . . extended by the American Constitution." The group survived until 1929.

Now the U.S. government wanted warmer relations with its neighbors to the south. Herbert Hoover, the U.S. secretary of commerce, recommended withdrawing all marines from Latin America. This view was taken up by the Democratic Party and made part of its political platform.

Latinos in the 1920s

6

After World War I ended, Congress intended to put an end to easy immigration for Mexicans. However, business owners put pressure on politicians to allow Mexicans to continue entering the United States. As a result, large numbers of Mexican immigrants continued to arrive, pulled by the promise of better economic opportunities. At the same time, another revolution in Mexico pushed other immigrants to move north. In the 1920s, Mexican immigration made up about 11 percent of all U.S. immigration. Most of the new arrivals at this time were peasants and farmers, although some were middle- and upper-class political refugees, fleeing the violence of the new revolution.

Many of the new arrivals headed to California. During the 1920s, the Mexican population of Los Angeles more than tripled. Others headed to the Midwest. In the 1920s, the Mexican population of the region grew by more than 600 percent, with most newcomers settling in the urban areas of Chicago and Detroit.

Small numbers of Cubans also continued to immigrate to the United States. In the 1920s, a group of young intellectuals fled to Miami. Here, they plotted against Cuba's dictator,

OPPOSITE The Corpus Christi, Texas, branch of the Sons of America (SOA) poses in 1929. The SOA was a veterans' group formed by Mexicans to help Mexican immigrants to the United States.

Gerardo Machado. Their efforts would pay off during the Great Depression, when they helped to overthrow Machado's U.S.-supported government. Another spurt of immigration from Cuba took place in 1928, when a major hurricane wiped out the island's coffee plantations. Many who had worked on the plantations decided to take their chances in the United States.

Latino Labor

In the coming years, Latinos helped build the nation. Mexican labor was in demand in field and factory alike. One industry that employed large numbers of Mexican workers was the railroads. By 1929, three out of every four railway workers with the six largest U.S. railways were Mexican.

More Latino women went to work than ever before. They worked on farms, in textile mills, at food processing plants, and in domestic service as maids and housekeepers. Latino women quickly found that they were doubly discriminated against. They were paid less than both Anglo women and Latino men.

Latino laborers faced a truly hostile working environment. Not only were they paid lower wages, but they often worked under unsafe, unsanitary conditions. Even though they performed jobs other workers did not want, they earned the resentment of whites and other immigrant workers. Many of the labor unions that protected U.S. workers were not willing to help Latino workers and refused to accept them as members. Other unions set up segregated locals, or branches, for Latinos only.

In the 1920s, Latinos began organizing their own unions, especially in agriculture. Latino miners also banded together to protect their rights. Many of these groups were supported or sponsored by the radical Industrial Workers of the World (IWW). The IWW was a socialist group that wanted to overthrow capitalism in the United States. The group used strikes, sabotage, and boycotts to try to accomplish this goal. Unlike the American Federation of Labor (AFL), the IWW encouraged unskilled Latino workers to join. However, Latino unions would only really gain in strength and power after the Great Depression.

Latino Communities

At this time, many Puerto Ricans came to the United States. In 1910, before the passage of the Jones Act, only about 1,500 Puerto Rican–born people lived in the United States. By 1930, the Puerto Rican population had skyrocketed, with more than 52,500 Puerto Ricans living on the mainland. Many of the new arrivals

Trouble in Texas

In the early 1920s, while the rest of the U.S. economy boomed, the Texas oil industry slumped. As job opportunities in several Texas towns dwindled, citizens tried to oust Mexican workers who had taken jobs in the oil fields during World War I. In Ranger, Texas, Anglos wearing masks destroyed the shacks that Mexican workers lived in. When the 600 workers turned to town officials to protect them, they were ordered to get out of town. In other Texas towns, Mexicans were threatened and attacked with rocks.

settled in Brooklyn, the Bronx, and East Harlem in New York City. In the coming years, these barrios would continue to attract Latino immigrants.

In the 1920s, Puerto Ricans began moving into East Harlem, a neighborhood that would eventually become one of the largest and most important Puerto Rican communities in the United States. In the late 1800s, East Harlem had been home to the largest Italian community in the nation. As more Puerto Ricans moved into the city, the area became known as El Barrio and Spanish Harlem. Even today, the neighborhood has a sizable Puerto Rican population. In neighborhoods such as El Barrio, new arrivals were able to hold on to their Puerto Rican cultural identity.

As did Mexican immigrants, newly arrived Puerto Ricans and Cubans formed mutual-aid groups. Many of these groups were known as *hermandades*, or brotherhoods. Such groups were based on people's social standing, area of birth, and even race. For example, Cubans of African descent were usually not allowed to join other Cuban or Spanish mutualistas; instead, they formed their own, such as the *Sociedad Martí-Maceo*. Merchants and workers often banded together to form their own associations.

Some Puerto Rican immigrants joined political groups like Club Borinquen. The goal of such groups was to advocate for Puerto Rican independence. Some political associations published newspapers, such as *El Porvenir (The Future)* and *La*

Fast Fact

During the 1920s, more than half of all Mexicans lived in urban areas. The top urban destination was Los Angeles. In 1925, Los Angeles had the largest Mexican population outside Mexico City. Just five years later, one out of every five residents there was Mexican.

Revolución (The Revolution). Thanks to their status as U.S. citizens, Puerto Ricans quickly became involved in U.S. politics. *La Liga Puertorriquena,* or the Puerto Rican League, was an organization of community associations that supported the Democratic Party.

By 1930, the Mexican-born population in the United States had grown to 1,400,000. Most Mexican immigrants still chose Texas and California as destinations. By 1930, four out of ten Mexican-born U.S. residents lived in Texas, while three out of ten lived in California. California was quickly becoming the most popular destination for Latino immigrants.

Dealing with Prejudice

As Mexican immigration increased in the 1920s, prejudice, segregation, and discrimination, especially in the Southwest, also grew. Labor unions, civic organizations, and nativists—people who favored native-born U.S. citizens over immigrants—all complained that the new immigrants put a burden on the existing economy by taking jobs and using social services. All these groups demanded that restrictions be placed on immigration from Mexico.

Other immigrant groups also discriminated against the newest Mexican arrivals, especially in the factories of the Northeast and the Midwest. Established groups like Italians and Poles did not want the Mexicans competing with them for jobs. Even people of Mexican descent discriminated against the new arrivals. As a result of the influx of mostly illiterate and poor Mexicans, many people of Mexican ancestry already in the United States began referring to

Signs like the one in this picture were common in the Southwest during the 1920s and throughout the Depression of the 1930s.

themselves as "Spanish" or "Spanish-American," as opposed to "Mexican" or "Mexican-American." The shift showed a new attitude—established Mexican Americans separated themselves from the same cultural identity of the new arrivals.

Latinos in the Southwest suffered from the same types of open discrimination that blacks in the Southeast did. The sign "No Mexicans Allowed" was common throughout the region. Latinos were banned from eating in Anglo restaurants, swimming in Anglo pools, and drinking from Anglo water fountains. They were forced to sit in special "colored" sections in movie theaters. Some communities prohibited Mexicans from living in Anglo neighborhoods.

Physical violence against Mexicans was also common in the Southwest. Killings along the border by the Texas Rangers continued, although the outcry over such abuse had already led to a reduction in the group's size in 1921. At this time, it was well known that no all-white jury in Texas would convict a Ranger for killing a Mexican. Such abuse of power would continue into the 1930s.

The Ku Klux Klan, a racist hate group that terrorized blacks and other minorities in the South, spread through the Southwest in the 1920s. The Klan was especially successful in Texas, where it numbered as many as 40,000 members at one point. In mining towns and farming communities, the Klan harassed and intimidated Mexican workers.

Unequal Education

The number of Latino children in public schools grew steadily. As a nation, the United States was now more willing to build schools and make sure that all children received an education. In addition, children's advocates were forcing officials to strictly enforce school attendance and child labor laws. In New Mexico, nearly three out of every four Latino children between the ages of five and 17 were enrolled in public schools. In Texas, the number had increased from 18 percent to nearly 50 percent, and it was 58 percent in California.

Many of these children were second-generation U.S. citizens, born in the United States to Mexican immigrants. The children were citizens both by birth and culture. They had less desire than their parents to maintain a bond with their homeland. They grew up surrounded by Anglos who could not understand their culture and ridiculed their accented speech. To fit in, they had to adapt to the ways of the United States. Lamented one Mexican: "How sorrowfully I have seen little children of Mexicans who could neither read nor write Spanish. They know that their parents are Mexican because they have heard it from the lips of others, but never from their own parents."

During the 1920s, education for Mexican children continued to be segregated and inferior to the education given to Anglo children. In southern California, for example, eight out of ten school districts at this time enrolled Mexicans and Mexican Americans in segregated schools.

One of the first things all Latino schoolchildren learned was that they must speak only English. Teachers in most schools discouraged the speaking of Spanish, and in some schools with English-only rules, Spanish was strictly forbidden. The goal of all schools at this time was to completely assimilate immigrant children.

Latino children were bullied or snubbed by some of their classmates. One Mexican student remembered being called names and shunned by classmates: "In grammar school they used to call us 'dirty Mexicans,' 'pelados' [tramps or bums], and greasers. A few times they moved away from me."

Beginning in 1925, Latino students were regularly excluded from secondary and further education. Because many Latino students spoke primarily Spanish, they were often labeled by teachers as "inferior, retarded, [and] learning-disabled." They would be put into slower-learning classes that focused on life and job skills, socialization, and assimilation instead of the academic subjects that would allow them to advance to secondary school. This practice started in the 1920s but became more pronounced in later years. In some cases, Latinos were not allowed to attend local high schools, which excluded them from later attending college. At this time, few colleges in the United States recruited Latino students.

The children of migrant workers were especially at risk of receiving little or no education. Because their families moved from place to place looking for work, these students attended many different schools. This made learning difficult at best. Some schools would not allow children to attend if their parents were migrant workers.

As a result of these hardships, Latino children were more likely than Anglo children to drop out of school. In Texas during the 1920s, about three out of every four Latino school-children withdrew from school by the third grade.

Immigration Laws

Under pressure from nativists, immigration laws tightened during the 1920s. In 1921 and 1924, Congress passed laws aimed at encouraging immigration from northern Europe and discouraging migration from Asia. The new laws instituted quotas, or limits, on the number of people allowed into the United States each year from certain countries. The laws temporarily ended immigration from Asia.

People like nativist politician John C. Box of Texas were not satisfied with the new laws. Box and others wanted to curb or end migra-tion from Mexico. Yet these laws did not include quotas on migration from the Western Hemisphere. Business owners in farming, mining,

John C. Box

One of the most outspoken opponents of Mexican immigration was Texas congressman John C. Box (1871–1941). A native of Texas, Box served in the House of Representatives from 1919 to 1931. In 1920, he said,

Americans found they could not live with [Mexicans] on genial terms in Texas 80 years ago. In a contest which arose then the Mexican showed both his inferior-ity and savage nature. The same traits which prevailed with them in the days of the Alamo . . . show themselves in dealings with each other and with the Americans now.

Box also criticized the fruit growers who wanted to keep immigration from Mexico open. He stated before Congress that these growers "want to bring the most ignorant, who are most easily handled 'like cattle.'"

and other industries put pressure on Congress to leave their labor pool alone. Said one fruit grower, "We want the Mexican because we can treat them as we cannot treat any other living man. . . . We can control them by keeping them at night behind bolted gates, within a stockade eight feet [2.4 m] high, surrounded by barbed wire. . . . We can make them work under armed guards in the fields."

As the pool of unskilled labor from other countries decreased as a result of the laws, Mexican and Puerto Rican labor was in even greater demand than before. Immigration from both countries increased as U.S. industries actively recruited labor. Puerto Ricans were particularly in demand, especially in the Northeast. Because of their status as U.S. citizens, they could move to the mainland with few problems. By 1930, the number of Puerto Ricans on the mainland had skyrocketed to about 53,000. Most were in New York.

Even though they were not excluded by the immigration quotas, Mexicans did not have an easy time crossing the border. To enter the United States legally, Mexicans had to show identification and other documents. They were now required to pay a $10 fee on top of the $8 head tax. This made it harder for the poor to cross.

The U.S. Border Patrol

To stem illegal immigration from Mexico, the United States established the U.S. Border Patrol in 1924. Before this time, the border was watched by Texas Rangers and military troops in training. Now, 450 full-time agents were employed to patrol the 2,000-mile (3,200 km) border between the two countries. Some of the first officers were former Texas Rangers. These men usually patrolled the border on horseback, although some used cars or trucks. They were paid $1,680 a year and given a badge and a revolver. They were, however, expected to provide their own horse and saddle.

In the late 1920s, U.S. and state officials began enforcing immigration requirements for Mexicans more strictly. The literacy test, created by Congress in 1917, was now used to weed out illiterate would-be immigrants. Documents were carefully checked and fees were collected. In 1929, Texas passed the Texas Emigrant Agent Law, banning out-of-state recruitment of workers.

As a result, legal immigration nearly ceased, while illegal immigration became more widespread than ever. At this time, professional smugglers became more common. For a fee, the smugglers hid Mexicans in cars or trucks and took them across the border illegally. Others immigrants entered illegally by wading across the Rio Grande at places where no checkpoints existed.

Around this time, racist views of the immigrants were expressed openly. For example, the derogatory term *wetback* was first used to describe these illegal immigrants because they entered the United States across the Rio Grande. Such views were voiced openly even by public officials. Wrote one U.S. customs agent, "It is a fact, also, and an unfortunate one so far as moral texture of Texas border communities is concerned, that the annual immigration tide from the southern Republic leaves upon our doorstep a horde of low-caste Mexicans—ignorant, immoral and unassimilable."

Advocacy Groups for Latinos

After World War I, Latino veterans returned home with a determination to be treated fairly. Second-generation Latinos began to identify as U.S. citizens, not as

Mexicans. These citizens expected to be treated like other U.S. citizens.

The result was an increase in the number of Latino self-help and advocacy groups during the 1920s. The number of mutualistas jumped during this decade, with one in nearly every U.S. barrio. San Antonio alone had 20 mutualistas.

One of the most important groups to get its start in the 1920s was the League of United Latin American Citizens (LULAC). Founded in 1929, LULAC fought for Latinos in the United States while at the same time encouraging them to assimilate into U.S. culture. The group's membership was mostly conservative, middle-class Texans of Mexican ancestry. LULAC would be a great help to Latinos during the coming economic depression.

Some groups changed focus. *La Liga Protectora Mexicana,* founded in 1917 by Manuel Gonzales, originally focused on securing fair legal treatment for Mexicans. Members of the group paid annual dues that were used to

In 1935, members of LULAC posed for this photo. Their motto was "All for one and one for all."

hire lawyers when needed. In 1920, however, the group changed its goal to preparing Mexican immigrants for the U.S. citizenship test. Gonzales resigned in protest.

Communications in the Latino Community

In the mid-1920s, Latinos began using radio to transmit news and information to the Spanish-speaking community. At first, Spanish broadcasters purchased airtime from Anglo stations. To pay for the time, they raised money by selling advertisements.

One pioneer in Latino radio was singer Pedro J. González. In the late 1920s and early 1930s, González broadcast a show called *Los Madrugadores* or *The Early Birds.* The program, aimed at Latino workers as they started their day, ran from four to six in the morning in Los Angeles. The station's strong radio signal allowed the show to be heard all over the Southwest, sometimes as far as Texas.

Each morning, thousands of Mexicans tuned in to hear González singing with his band and talking about the politics of the time. His progressive views on politics eventually got him into trouble. He was falsely charged with rape in 1934 and sent to San Quentin Prison for six years. Some people believe that González was framed for the crime by L.A. officials who were unhappy with the broadcaster's outspoken views on immigration. After his release, González was deported to Mexico.

The Great Depression

7

I n late 1929, the United States faced some of its darkest days ever. On October 29, the New York Stock Exchange crashed, costing citizens millions of dollars. "Black Tuesday," as the date became known, marked the beginning of the Great Depression. This severe economic crisis, which would spread to other industrialized nations around the world, lasted into the early 1940s.

During the Depression, banks, factories, and other businesses closed down. Millions of people lost their jobs, their life savings, and their homes. People stood for hours on bread lines and in front of soup kitchens to get food for themselves and their families.

In the early 1930s, residents of the Great Plains of the Midwest also faced a severe drought. Winds blowing across the plains lifted the dry topsoil, creating huge dust storms and making the area uninhabitable. Thousands of farmers left the Midwest and moved to Texas and California, searching for work.

OPPOSITE Thousands of workers, including many Latinos, lost their jobs during the Great Depression. This group marched through the streets of Washington, D.C., demanding aid from the government in 1932.

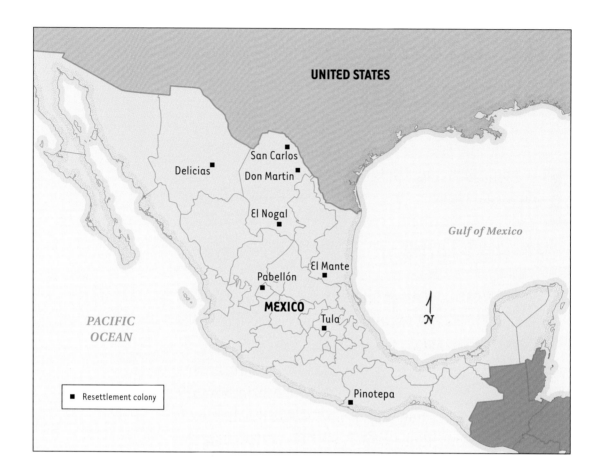

During the Great Depression, Mexicans in the United States who were repatriated back to Mexico often settled in the colonies indicated on this map.

The Great Depression took a toll on all people in the United States, but Mexican immigrants were especially hard-hit. As the economy soured, more and more people in the United States lashed out at Latino workers, using them as scapegoats. They blamed the immigrants for taking factory, mining, railroad, and other jobs away from "real Americans." Companies were pressured to fire the Latinos and hire out-of-work whites and blacks.

Mexicans working in the farming industry also suffered. In 1930, 41 percent of all Mexicans in the United States worked in farming. In the late 1920s, eight out of every ten farm workers were of Mexican descent. Like other U.S. farmers, especially in the Dust Bowl of the Midwest and in drought-stricken New Mexico, Mexican-Americans lost their jobs, and many headed to California. Now that cheap labor was available everywhere, they soon found that farms preferred to hire whites. Other displaced Mexican immigrants migrated to big cities, but jobs there were just as difficult to get.

Reverse Migration and Repatriation

During the 1930s, more Mexicans exited the United States than entered it. As the Depression worsened, some chose to return to their native land. Others were pressured by local officials and citizens in their region. U.S. residents throughout the Southwest angrily blamed Mexican immigrants for taking jobs and public aid. During the first years of the Depression, about one out of every four left the United States.

As the United States struggled in the grip of the Great Depression, nativist groups began calling for repatriation programs. The goal of such programs was to send home Mexicans who were living in the United States without legal documentation.

Mexicans became the target of propaganda and publicity campaigns to arouse national anti-immigration sentiment. In Los Angeles, the Citizens Committee for Coordination for Unemployment Relief wrote about Mexicans, "We need their jobs for needy citizens." The group stated that about 400,000 "deportable aliens" were living in Los Angeles County.

In response, President Herbert Hoover initiated a repatriation program to deport Mexican-born people to Mexico. Those who would not leave willingly were deported by the U.S. Immigration Service. As a result of the repatriation program, about 500,000 Latinos left the United States.

The Mexicans who were being repatriated were rounded up by local agencies, herded into boxcars like cattle, and left at Mexican towns just south of the U.S.-Mexican border. In California, detention camps were built to house Mexicans awaiting deportation.

State, county, and local officials also used repatriation programs and other means to encourage Mexicans to leave the country. In 1931, for example, California began banning noncitizens from working on public works projects. In California, Texas, and Colorado, Mexicans were refused welfare if they would not leave the United States.

Although the idea behind the programs was to deport illegal aliens, many Mexican Americans were also forced out of the country. When a family member faced deportation, that person's spouse and children had to decide whether to remain alone in the United States or follow their loved one to Mexico. As a result, many U.S.-born children who had been brought up speaking English were now forced to adapt to a new Spanish-speaking culture. These displaced Latinos were often looked down upon by their new neighbors in Mexico, who labeled them *Norteños*, or northerners.

Fast Fact

Between 1930 and 1939, one-sixth of all people of Mexican descent in the United States were repatriated to Mexico. More than half of those repatriated had been born in the United States, which made them U.S. citizens. In 1932 alone, about 200,000 Mexicans were repatriated.

The repatriation program wiped out once-thriving barrios. Latino shops and businesses closed down. Civic groups fell apart as community leaders were deported. Families were forced to leave behind their land and homes, which were sometimes sold to pay for their transportation back to Mexico. The program encouraged a deep distrust of the U.S. federal government.

Cubans and Puerto Ricans during the Depression

In Cuba, the Great Depression weakened the dictatorship of the U.S.-supported leader Gerardo Machado. When his government was overthrown by workers and students, he and his supporters fled to Florida and sought political asylum there. In the coming years, political refugees from Cuba would continue to flee to Miami and other cities in Florida. However, Cuban immigration to the United States would not truly pick up until after 1959, when communist leader Fidel Castro took power in Cuba.

In Puerto Rico, a hurricane in 1932 nearly destroyed the island's ailing coffee industry. As a result, people continued to move from Puerto Rico to the mainland. Despite the Great Depression, the number of Puerto Ricans in the United States grew by more than 17,000 in the 10-year period between 1930 and 1940. The top destination continued to be New York City.

Latino culture in the Southwest suffered as many Mexicans returned to Mexico—voluntarily or otherwise. In the Northeast, with no forced repatriation of Cubans and Puerto Ricans, Latino cultural life continued to flourish.

New Puerto Rican newspapers were founded at this time, and Puerto Rican playwrights, novelists, and poets published their work during and after the Depression.

Fighting for Fairness

In 1932, at the height of the Great Depression, Franklin Delano Roosevelt was elected as the 32nd president of the United States. In his inaugural address, Roosevelt unveiled his Good Neighbor Policy. This new policy signaled an official shift of attitudes and practices towards Latin America. In the coming years, U.S. Marines were withdrawn from Latin American nations. The year after Roosevelt's inauguration, the Platt Amendment, which had allowed the United States to intervene in Cuban affairs, was annulled.

Roosevelt's chief concern during his first term as president was to bring the Great Depression to an end. Soon after he took office, he called Congress into special session to start working on the New Deal, a plan of relief and reform.

Many of Roosevelt's New Deal policies were aimed specifically at Latinos. Democrats in Congress quickly put an end to the Mexican repatriation programs. These politicians knew that Latinos were not to blame for the Depression, and they believed that deportation solved none of the United States' problems. They also created such groups as the Works Progress Administration (WPA), the Civilian Conservation Corps, and the National Youth Administration. These agencies provided jobs for all people, regardless of their ancestry.

The Works Progress Art Project (WPAP), for example, hired Latino artists during the Depression to paint murals in government buildings throughout the nation. Most of these murals depicted community themes, such as a town's pioneers or its most important industry.

Another project that employed Latinos during the Depression was the Federal Theater Project, a program meant to give out-of-work actors and theater people employment. A Spanish-language branch of the project was headquartered in Tampa during 1936 and 1937. The project presented integrated shows featuring both Latino and Anglo actors. However, these shows were not successful because many non-Latinos in Tampa refused to attend shows at the Centro Asturiano. In 1937, the Latino branch lost 25 members when Congress passed a law that removed foreigners from the WPA.

Muralist Diego Rivera, whose work served as an inspiration for President Franklin Roosevelt's WPA program, is shown painting *Detroit Industry* in 1932 at the Detroit Institute of Art.

Righting Old Wrongs

The repatriation programs sparked a movement among Latinos to fight harder for fair and equal treatment in the United States. Around this time, Mexican Americans began using the term *La Raza*, which means "the race" or "the people," to refer to themselves and their culture with pride.

The number of Latino clubs in the United States grew. Some of these groups believed that the more "Americanized" their members were, the more accepted they would be in U.S. society. Such groups as LULAC encouraged their members to take up U.S. ways and give up Latino culture.

One of the most influential and well-known Latino politicians was Dennis Chávez. Chávez was born in Los Chavez, New Mexico, in 1888. He was forced to leave school after the seventh grade and go to work delivering groceries to help support his family. As a young man, Chávez became active in politics. In 1916, he took a job as a clerk for New Mexico's Democratic U.S. senator in Washington, D.C. He worked during the day while studying at night to earn his law degree.

Chávez returned home to New Mexico and started his own law practice. In 1930, he won a seat in the U.S. House of Representatives. In 1934, he ran for the Senate but narrowly lost. When his opponent was killed in an airplane crash, New Mexico's governor appointed him to the seat. In 1936, he was elected by state voters, becoming the first Latino elected to serve a full term in the U.S. Senate.

Throughout his career, Chávez fought for the rights of Latinos and other minorities. As chair of the Public Works Committee, he gained federal funds for irrigation and other important projects in New Mexico. Chávez died in 1962.

Strikes of the 1930s

During the 1930s, thousands of Mexican and other immigrant workers went on strike, protesting the terrible conditions under which they worked. Many of the strikes were in the agricultural industry. Throughout the 1930s, unions organized strikes of Mexican farm workers, especially in California. Immigrants working in fruit orchards and in melon, strawberry, celery, and cotton fields all took part in organized strikes.

The year 1933 was an important one for farm workers, who staged 50 strikes throughout the course of the year. The biggest strike took place in the Central Valley, a major cotton-farming region in California. Since the beginning of the Depression, farm owners had drastically cut the wages of their workers, from one dollar to 40 cents for every 100 pounds (45 kg) of cotton picked. In October, 1,800 workers walked off the fields with the encouragement of several independent unions. Three out of four of the workers were Mexican.

Throughout the 20th century, Latino farm workers such as these Mexicans, shown in Texas in 1959, have had to fight for better pay and working conditions.

Farm owners retaliated by throwing the workers out of company-owned camps. Then the owners called in the police and armed Anglo citizens to intimidate the striking workers. Strike leaders were arrested, and two strikers were killed in the struggle. After 24 days on strike, the workers were given a wage increase to 75 cents for every 100 pounds of cotton picked.

One female labor leader who was active in the 1930s was Luisa Moreno. Born in Guatemala in 1906, Moreno moved to the United States with her Mexican husband in

1928. In New York, she found work as a seamstress at a garment factory that employed Latino women—many from Puerto Rico. After witnessing the terrible working conditions firsthand, Moreno helped women organize labor unions within garment factories throughout the city. She later helped organize unions and strikes in cigar factories and pecan-shelling plants.

Moreno was also a civil rights pioneer. In 1939, she organized the first *Congreso de Pueblos de Habla Espanola,* or Congress of Spanish-Speaking People. The congress marked the first time that anyone had attempted to unite all Latino Americans across the United States, regardless of their country of origin. Those who attended the congress, held in Los Angeles, wanted to improve housing, working conditions, and educational opportunities for Latino Americans. They also believed in preserving Latino culture in the United States. The congress lasted until 1945, and at its strongest had 874,000 dues-paying members. In 1950, Moreno was deported as a "dangerous alien."

Puerto Rican Independence Movements

While Mexican and other Latino workers were fighting for their rights in the 1930s, Puerto Ricans also had another cause to work toward—independence for Puerto Rico. In the late 1930s the *independentistas*, as those in favor of a free Puerto Rico were called, were led by Dr. Pedro Albizu Campos. Campos, who called himself "the president of the Puerto Rican Republic," gave fiery speeches throughout

Latin America in an attempt to gather support.

Between 1937 and 1947, Campos was imprisoned in the United States for attempting to overthrow the government. In Puerto Rico, supporters marched in Ponce, his hometown, to protest the verdict. Police opened fire on the crowd, killing more than 20 marchers and wounding 100. In the coming decades, those favoring an independent Puerto Rico would resort to acts of violence on both the island and the mainland.

Some U.S. residents on the mainland agreed that Puerto Rico should be autonomous. In 1936 and 1937, bills were introduced into Congress asking for Puerto Rican independence. Both failed. The majority of members of Congress believed that economic and social conditions on the island needed to improve before independence could be considered.

During the first four decades of the 20th century, the population of Latinos in the United States increased. Latinos began migrating out of the Southwest in large groups for the first time during this period, and they made some strides toward fairer treatment across the nation. However, the real breakthrough for Latino Americans would come in the second part of the century, beginning with World War II in 1942.

A Belated Apology

On January 1, 2006, California offered an apology to all Mexicans who were repatriated during the 1930s. In addition to the official apology, a monument will be placed in a Los Angeles park to commemorate the event. However, the apology stopped short of offering to repay any who may have suffered financially as a result of the program.

Timeline

1898	The Teller Amendment prevents the United States from annexing Cuba. The United States acquires Guam, Puerto Rico, and the Philippines from Spain. Cuba becomes an independent nation, but the United States controls its economy and government.
1910	The Mexican Revolution begins, spurring widespread immigration into the United States.
1916	Mexican revolutionary Pancho Villa attacks towns along the U.S.-Mexican border, fueling anti-Mexican sentiment in the region.
1917	The Zimmerman note proposes a German-Mexican alliance against the United States. Congress passes an immigration act that requires all immigrants to read and write at least one language. The Jones Act gives U.S. citizenship to Puerto Ricans. The United States enters World War I.
1921	New immigration laws result in an increased demand for cheap labor from Mexico.
1929	The Great Depression begins.
1930	U.S., state, and local officials begin programs to repatriate Mexicans to Mexico.
1934	The Platt Amendment is annulled.
1936	A bill introduced into Congress for Puerto Rican independence fails. Dennis Chávez becomes the first Latino elected to serve a full term in the U.S. Senate.
1939	Luisa Moreno organizes the first Congreso de Pueblos de Habla Espanola, or Congress of Spanish-Speaking People.
1942	World War II begins.

Glossary

assimilate To fit into a new society or culture.

autonomy Self-government, independence.

barrio A Latino neighborhood.

colonia A town or community founded by Latino workers.

corrido A type of Mexican folk ballad sung to polka, waltz, or march music.

enganchista A Mexican-American labor contractor hired to find Mexican workers and transport them illegally across the border.

independentista A person who favored Puerto Rican independence.

Latin America The countries of the Western Hemisphere south of the United States, especially those in which the main language is Spanish.

mutualista A self-help society founded by Latino immigrants that offered health and life insurance, death benefits, and financial aid in times of trouble.

nativist A person who favored native-born U.S. residents over immigrants.

protectorate A nation that is protected by a larger, more powerful one.

repatriation The act of sending someone back to his or her country of origin.

strike The organized act of stopping work in order to force an employer to improve working conditions.

subsistence farming The growing of food crops to feed a family or community, not to sell for profit.

vaqueros Latino cattle drivers or cowboys.

Further Reading

Books

Amparano, Julie. *America's Latinos: Their Rich History, Culture, and Traditions.* Chanhassen, MN: Child's World, 2003.

Englar, Mary. *Pancho Villa: Rebel of the Mexican Revolution.* Mankato, MN: Fact Finders, 2006.

Hunter, Amanda. *Latino Americans and Immigration Laws: Crossing the Border.* Philadelphia: Mason Crest, 2005.

Kanellos, Nicholás. *Great Hispanic Americans.* Lincolnwood, IL: Publications International, 2005.

Ochoa, George. *Atlas of Hispanic-American History.* New York: Checkmark Books, 2001.

Web Sites

The Chicana/Chicano Experience in Arizona,
http://www.asu.edu/lib/archives/website/index.htm

Five Views: An Ethnic Historic Site Survey for California; A History of Mexican Americans in California: Revolution to Depression: 1900–1940,
http://www.cr.nps.gov/history/online_books/5views/5views5c.htm

Hispanic Heritage Plaza,
http://www.hispaniconline.com/hh04/index.html

Hispanic Reading Room,
http://www.loc.gov/rr/hispanic/

Bibliography

Books

Davis, Mike. *Magical Urbanism: Latinos Reinvent the US City.* New York: Verso, 2000.

Gertz, Lynne Marie. *Schools of Their Own: The Education of Hispanos in New Mexico.* Albuquerque: University of New Mexico Press, 1997.

Martínez, Oscar. *Mexican-Origin People in the United States.* Tucson: University of Arizona Press, 2001.

Rosales, F. Arturo. *Chicano! The History of the Mexican American Civil Rights Movement.* Houston, TX: Arte Público Press, 1996.

Ruiz, Vicki L., and Virginia Sánchez Korrol. *Latina Legacies: Identity, Biography, and Community.* New York: Oxford University Press, 2005.

Web Sites

Arizona State University. "The Chicana/Chicano Experience in Arizona." URL: http://www.asu.edu/lib/archives/website/index.htm. Downloaded on April 11, 2006.

The Library of Congress. "Hispanic Reading Room." URL: http://www.loc.gov/rr/hispanic/. Downloaded on April 11, 2006.

The Library of Congress. "Puerto Rico at the Dawn of the Modern Age." URL: http://memory.loc.gov/ammem/collections/puertorico/bras.html. Downloaded on June 1, 2006.

The Texas State Historical Society Online. "The Handbook of Texas Online: Texas Rangers." URL: http://www.tsha.utexas.edu/handbook/online/articles/TT/met4.html. Downloaded on June 1, 2006.

102

Index

Note: Page numbers in *italics* indicate photographs or illustrations. Page numbers followed by m indicate maps. Page numbers followed by g indicate glossary entries. Page numbers in **boldface** indicate box features.

advocacy groups 83–85, *84. See also* mutualista
agriculture. *See* farming
Allen, Charles H. (governor of Puerto Rico) 20
Allied Powers 63–64, 68
American Federation of Labor (AFL) 75
American Indians **5**, 9
American Legion 71
Aparicio, Manuel **54**
apology **97**
Arango, Doroteo. *See* Villa, Francisco "Pancho" (Doroteo Arango)
Arizona
    colonias in 42
    mutualista in 44, *72*
    strike in 35, 37
arts, Latino 51–52, *52*
Asia, immigration from 81
assimilate 99g
autonomy 99g
Azuela, Mariano 47

B
Barbosa, José Celso (Puerto Rican leader) *18*, 18
Barkley, David Bennes 67
barrio 42–43, 91, 99g
baseball, Latinos in 56–57, *58*, **58**, 59
"big stick" policy *12*, 16–17
Box, John C. 81, **81**
boxing **57**
Brooklyn Navy Yard 66

C
Caballo, León 31
Cajas, Juan Emilio Viguié 61
California
    Latino immigrants in 73, 77
    Latinos in movies 59–61
    Mexican population in Los Angeles 76
    repatriation apology **97**
    repatriation from 89–90

strikes in 35–36, 95
California Commission on Immigration and Housing 36
Campos, Pedro Albizu 96–97
canción-corrido (Latino song) 50, **50**
Cansino, Margarita Carmen (Rita Hayworth) 60
Carpa García (tent show) 54
carpas 54
Casa Editorial Lozano 47
Central Powers 63–64
Centro Asturiano theater (Tampa, Florida) 55, 93
Chávez, Dennis (Latino politician) 94
children
    education of 41–42, 79–81
    Latino family 43
    mutualista education for 44
    work of 33, 34
Cinco de Mayo 43
Citizens Committee for Coordination for Unemployment Relief 89
civil rights
    Congreso Mexicanista **36**
    of Latinos after World War I 71
    of Latinos in U.S. 30
    Latinos struggle for equality 35–37
    Luisa Moreno and 96
Civilian Conservation Corps 92
class system 33
Clifton, Arizona 35
Club Borinquen 76
Cody, Buffalo Bill 56
colonia 42, 99g
Colorado 36–37
Colorado Fuel & Oil Company 37
Columbia 51
Columbus, Christopher 9
communications, Latino 85
communities
    communications in 85
    Latino 75–77, **76**
    Mexican-American *42*, 42–43
    repatriation and 91
Congreso de Pueblos de Habla Espanola (Congress of Spanish-Speaking People) 96
Congreso Mexicanista (Mexican Congress) **36**

conjunto music (*música norteña*) 50
corrido (ballad) **50**, 50, 99g
cowboys *38*, 55–56
Cuba
    baseball in 56
    boxer from **57**
    Guantánamo naval base in **24**, *24*
    music of 51
    Spanish-American War over 13–15, *14*
    U.S. control of 15–16
    U.S. interference in 23, 25
Cubans
    in Great Depression 91
    immigration after World War I 73–74
    mutual-aid groups 76
culture, Latino
    arts 51–52, *52*
    dance *48*
    Latinos in movies 59–61, **60**
    music 49–51, **50**
    mutualista 43–45
    sports 55–59, *56*, **57**, *58*, **58**
    theater 52–55, **54**

D
Díaz, Porfirio (Mexican president) 27
Dihigo, Martín 57, **58**
discrimination
    Congreso Mexicanista and **36**
    against Latino immigrants 77–78, *78*, 83
    against Latino women 74
    against Latinos 30–33, *31*
    struggle for equality 35–37
    in U.S. military 67
disease 9
"dollar diplomacy" 17

E
East Harlem, New York 76
education 41–42, 79–81
El Heraldo de Brownsville (newspaper) 47
El Misisipí (newspaper) **46**
El Tiempo de Laredo (newspaper) 46
employment 6. *See also* work
enganchista 69–70, 99g
equality 35–37. *See also* civil rights
Escobar, Sixto **57**

About the Author

Robin Doak

Robin Doak holds a B.A. in English, with a concentration in journalism, from the University of Connecticut. She has worked for Weekly Reader Corporation as an editor and is currently a freelance writer who, over the last 10 years, has authored and coauthored 38 books, primarily educational reading material for children.

Mark Overmyer-Velázquez

Mark Overmyer-Velázquez, general editor and author of the preface included in each of the volumes, holds a BA in History and German Literature from the University of British Columbia, and MA, MPhil and PhDs in Latin American and Latino History from Yale University. While working on a new book project on the history of Mexican migration to the United States, he teaches undergraduate and graduate courses in Latin American and U.S. Latina/o history at the University of Connecticut.